EARLY TIMES
THE STORY OF ANCIENT GREECE

SECOND EDITION

Suzanne Strauss Art

(The Fay School, Southborough, Massachusetts)

WAYSIDE PUBLISHING

SUITE #5, 11 JAN SEBASTIAN WAY
SANDWICH, MASSACHUSETTS
TOLL FREE # (888) 302-2519
E-MAIL: wayside@sprintmail.com

To David

PRINTED IN THE UNITED STATES

ISBN 1-877653-26-8

Acknowledgements

I am very grateful for the continuing support and constructive criticism offered by two of my colleagues at the Fay School: Richard Upjohn of the History Department and Daniel Arnaud of Classics. Both men are extremely knowledgeable and perceptive scholars, and they generously devoted substantial amounts of time to reading, editing and commenting upon my manuscript. Dick and Dan, you personify the joyful spirit of inquiry that once propelled the ancient Greeks to geometrically expand their understanding of the universe and of man's place in it.

Many thanks also go to my students at Fay: They inspired me to create a series of history books that are relevant to the lives of middle schoolers and are fun to read. Their reactions to my sample chapters as well as their suggestions for activities helped me to produce books that are undeniably "kid-oriented."

Most of all, much love and appreciation go to my ever-patient family—my husband Bob and my children David and Robyn. They put up with many a late dinner as I worked for "just a few more minutes" at the computer.

To The Teacher

This book is geared toward middle school students (grades 5-8), and it can be used for either a unit or a year's study of ancient Greece. It is comprehensive in scope, covering the major historical periods from the Bronze Age to the Hellenistic Era and highlighting the evolution of political thought, economics, science, art and literature. At the same time, emphasis is placed upon detailed descriptions of everyday life as well as provocative portraits of key personalities in order to make the civilization of the early Greeks "come alive" for young readers.

The vocabulary is generally age appropriate for middle schoolers; however, a fair number of challenging words have been included to enliven the prose and to expand the students' mastery of the English language. At the same time, frequent references are made to the Greek "roots" from which so many of our words are derived.

Each chapter is followed by a set of questions to help the students review what they have read. "Ideas to Think About" provide materials for further discussion and/or enrichment activities. "Projects" are suggestions for independent as well as group assignments. The books listed in *Suggested Readings* are excellent resources for research projects, and their illustrations are very useful for enriching class discussions. I recommend that many of them be available in the classroom to students throughout their study of Greece.

THE STORY OF ANCIENT GREECE is the product of nine years of teaching experiences as well as a life-long fascination with the subject. The original manuscript was "test marketed" and refined in my own classroom, and the projects are based upon those activities my students enjoyed the most.

Contents

PART I — THE BRONZE AGE

PART II — ATHENS ACHIEVES GREATNESS

PART III — THE LATER YEARS

List of Maps, Charts and Diagrams

The photographs in this book have been reproduced with the permission of the Boston Museum of Fine Arts.

Drawings are by Evan Frank (F) and the author.

I. Maps

II. Charts and Diagrams

Timeline

note: c. is used to denote approximate dates. It comes from the Latin word "circa" which means "around." Thus c. 800 B.C. means around 800 B.C.

Neolithic Period   c. 4000 B.C. — Crete is settled

Bronze Age   c. 2000 B.C. — the Acheans settle in
                                  Greece
                             c. 1600-1450 — height of Minoan
                                  civilization
                             c. 1600-1100 B.C. — the Mycenean Age
                             c. 1200 B.C. — the fall of Troy
                                  1140 B.C. — the Dorian invasion

---

Dark Ages   776 B.C. — the first Olympic Games

Archaic Period   c. 750 B.C. — Homer
                             c. 720 B.C. — Greek alphabet in use
                             594 B.C. — Solon's Reforms
                             490-479 B.C. — Persian Wars

Classical Period   460-429 B.C. — Age of Pericles
                             431-404 B.C. — the Peloponnesian War
                             399 B.C. — death of Socrates
                             336-323 B.C. — era of Alexander the Great

---

Hellenistic Period   323-30 B.C.
                             Alexandria becomes a great center of
                                  learning
                             Greek culture spreads throughout
                                  Alexander's former empire

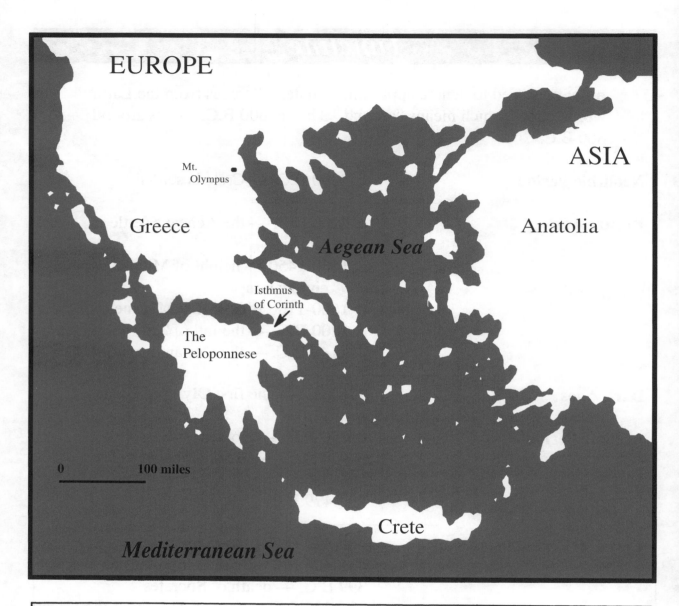

fig. 1 — **Greece and its surrounding regions**

INTRODUCTION

Twenty-four hundred years ago, a Greek statesman named Pericles delivered a dramatic speech honoring the soldiers who had recently fallen in battle and praising the city of Athens, in whose defense they had given their lives. "Future ages will wonder at us," he proclaimed, "as the present age wonders at us now."

Athens was indeed an exceptional city: It was the birthplace of democracy and the site of the richest flowering of artistic and intellectual activity the ancient world had ever known. Try to envision the civilization of ancient Greece as a giant constellation in the dark evening sky; among the many stars that sparkle and glisten, one is particularly brilliant. This bright star is Athens.

An inquisitive spirit and a supreme confidence in their own abilities set the Greeks apart from the other peoples of the early Mediterranean world. They were never burdened by an oppressive, centralized government like that of Egypt, and so they felt free to question and investigate anything they didn't understand. In an unprecedented flurry of experimentation and creativity that peaked in Athens in the fifth century B.C., the Greeks achieved great heights not only in political matters but also in the realms of mathematics, science, philosophy, art, architecture, literature, and theater.

Greece's Unique Geography

Greece is a mountainous peninsula in southeastern Europe that juts into the Mediterranean Sea. It is a relatively small nation, roughly the size of New York state, but its extremely ragged coastline is over two thousand miles long! Numerous bays and inlets contain quiet waters and make excellent natural harbors, and no part of the country is more than sixty miles from the coast. The sea played an important part in the economic and political development of Greece.

The land itself is divided into two major geographical areas of approximately the same size. The southern part, called the Peloponnese, looks like a giant hand grasping at the long offshore island of Crete. It is connected to the northern half of Greece by a narrow (four-mile wide) strip of land called the Isthmus of Corinth.

To the east of the Greek peninsula is the Aegean Sea, a part of the Mediterranean that separates Europe from Asia. Its calm blue waters are dotted with scenic islands that form stepping stones from Greece to the western projection of the continent of Asia (modern Turkey). In ancient times this small extension of Asia was called *Anatolia*, a Greek word meaning "the land where the sun rises."

Rugged mountains of limestone cover over three quarters of mainland Greece. The highest peak, Mt. Olympus, rises in the northeast 9,570 feet above sea level. This snow-capped and cloud-covered mountain played an important part in the religion and literature of the ancient Greeks. The mountains that line much of the coast appear to be higher than they actually are, because they plunge so steeply down to the sea. The only flat and arable (cultivable) land in southern Greece lies on the coastal plains and in the mountain valleys. A few of the valleys are connected by narrow passes, but most are completely surrounded by rocky peaks. In the north, the region of Thessaly has gently rolling hills ideal for pastures. Although there are no major rivers in Greece, mountain springs and cascading streams provide a plentiful supply of fresh water.

Originally the hillsides were heavily forested, but the ancient people cut down the trees to build houses and boats. The roots of the trees had held the soil in place; once they were gone, erosion depleted the land of its fertile top layer. This explains why from very early times most of the hillsides were more suitable for the grazing of sheep and goats than the cultivation of crops.

The Greek climate is similar to that of southern California. Seasonal winds from the Mediterranean bring moderate rainfall to the peninsula during the late fall and winter months, while the summers are very hot and dry. It seldom snows, except in the high mountains.

Greece is one of the most scenic countries in southern Europe. Try to imagine the rough contours of the mountains rising majestically above the green valleys, the sparkling blue surface of the sea breaking upon the shores, and the brightness of the summer sky that makes everything appear clean and crisp—don't these bounties of nature create a panorama of extraordinary beauty?

A Spirit of Independence

The geography of Greece had a great influence upon the rich civilization that evolved there over two thousand years ago. The early settlers built their villages in the sheltered valleys and coastal plains; the mountains and the sea formed imposing barriers that made travel difficult and isolated one community from another. As a result, each village had to depend upon its own resources to survive. Hard work and cooperative efforts enabled the settlers to forge a good living in a rather harsh environment, and this engendered in them a great sense of accomplishment and an enthusiasm for facing new challenges.

Occasionally problems arose that affected an entire village. At such times, the differing opinions of the leaders were all considered before a decision was agreed upon. The concept of a group of men making rules and regulations for the common good of the community was a revolutionary idea in the ancient world, where most people's lives were dictated by the whims of their kings and emperors. It eventually led to the creation of a form of government known as *democracy* (a Greek word meaning "rule by the people"). Today, most of the governments of the modern world are based upon the principles of democracy that were formulated in ancient Greece.

Curiosity Leads To Discovery

The Greeks were a very curious people; they carefully studied their environment and pondered the meanings of such phenomena as the movement of stars and the life cycles of plants and animals. At first they attributed all natural occurrences to the powers of supernatural beings, but over the centuries their careful observation and experimentation resulted in many important discoveries in science and mathematics. The Greeks marveled at their own powers of logic and reason, and they tried to determine where man fit into the grand scheme of the universe. Their fascination with the way human beings think and act led to the creation of the scholarly disciplines of history, philosophy and psychology.

A Rich Heritage

The Greeks' celebration of the human potential is reflected in the ancient statues and paintings that have been recovered by modern archaeologists. Their love of order and harmony can be seen in the elegant design of the remains of their buildings. Remnants of lyrical poetry and thoughtful essays written in those early times reveal hopes and dreams that are not so different from our own. The theater as we know it was invented by the Greeks, and many of their plays are enjoyed by modern audiences. Action-packed epics and fanciful myths dreamed up by highly imaginative Greek storytellers are still fun to read, and they are the source of such modern metaphors as "Achilles' heel," "Pandora's box," and "the face that launched a thousand ships."

Why Study the Ancient Greeks?

We owe so much to the Greeks! Their zealous appreciation of human life, their ardent pursuit of knowledge and their unbridled bursts of artistic and intellectual creativity continue to shine as a beacon of inspiration for the modern world. Indeed, their achievements form the cornerstones of our own culture. Where would we be without democracy, theater, and the spirit of the Olympic Games? Pericles was right when he predicted that future ages would wonder at the legacy of Athens!

By turning back the clock to those early times and delving into the everyday lives of the men, women, and children of ancient Greece, we can begin to envision the circumstances that produced their extraordinary civilization. At the same time, we can gain a better understanding of the underlying principles of our own culture. So let's begin!

Questions:

1. Who was Pericles?
2. Describe the general attitude that set the Greeks apart from other peoples of the ancient Mediterranean world.
3. What is the Peloponnese?
4. What is the highest mountain in Greece?
5. Describe Greece's climate.
6. How did the mountainous terrain influence the development of self-government in Greece?
7. What are some examples of Greek culture that are readily apparent in our modern world?
8. List five adjectives that describe the ancient Greeks.

Ideas to Think About:

1. Our knowledge of ancient Greece comes from many sources. Archaeologists have found (and continue to find) remains and artifacts that have been buried in the ground for millennia. Many of the ancient vases that have been recovered are decorated with paintings of scenes of everyday life in Greece. Ruins of ancient buildings such as the Parthenon in Athens are still standing. Also, many Greek statues were copied by Roman sculptors, and so even when the originals are lost, the copies often have survived. Greek

writers produced a great wealth of manuscripts; as with the statues, many of their writings were copied into other languages and have survived in that form.

2. *Peloponnese* is a Greek word that means "Pelops' island." According to legend, this land was once ruled by King Pelops, grandson of the god Zeus and father of King Atreus (more about them later!). Since the Peloponnese is connected to the mainland by only a narrow strip of land, the early people considered it a separate piece of land, an island. In 1893 a canal was cut through the isthmus, enabling "Pelop's island" to truly live up to its ancient name.

3. Even at the height of its civilization ancient Greece had a relatively small population (there were only about 40,000 Athenian citizens). If you examine a map of the world, Greece appears tiny and insignificant. It is astounding that such a small group of people could have had such a significant and long lasting effect upon western civilization. (see *fig. 2*)

4. The letters B.C. stand for "before Christ." Historians arbitrarily use the birth of Christ as a convenient point in time for dating events. Everything that occurred after that time is referred to as A.D., which stands for *Anno Domini* (Latin for "the year of our Lord"). The first hundred years after the birth of

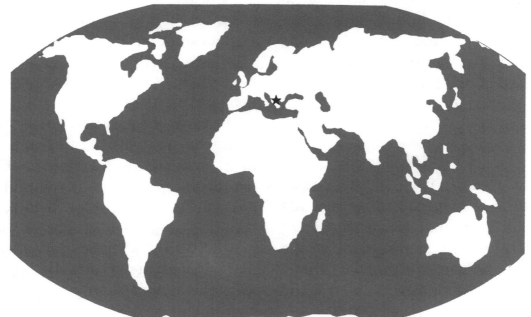

*fig. 2 — ***Greece's location on the world map**

(fig. 3) — **Timeline of dates B.C. and A.D.**

present time

A.D. 201 - 300	the third century A.D.
A.D. 101 - 200	the second century A.D.
A.D. 1 - 100	the first century A.D.

Birth of Christ

1 - 100 B.C.	the first century B.C.
101 - 200 B.C.	the second century B.C.
201 - 300 B.C.	the third century B.C.

prehistoric times

Christ make up the first century A.D.; the years from 101 to 200 make up the second century; and so on. We determine the dates B.C. by counting backwards. In other words, the years up to the hundredth one before Christ was born make up the first century B.C.; the years from 101 to 200 before he was born make up the second century B.C.; and so on. (see *fig. 3* above)

Projects:

1. Make a relief map of the Greek peninsula and surrounding islands using clay or instant paper mache. Paint the valleys and plains green, the mountains brown, and the water blue. Mt. Olympus should be painted white to indicate its snow cover.

2. Grapes and olives became the major crops of Greece. Find out how these plants are grown. What sort of soil and how much moisture do they require? Why was the natural environment of Greece so ideal for their cultivation? Write a short report.

3. Geography plays an important role in the development of any culture. The mountains of Greece fostered the isolation of communities and made them independent. Imagine that Greece had no mountains at all. Would there have been many rulers or only one? How independent would each community have been? Write a paragraph describing the kind of government that probably would have evolved in a country that was flat and open.

PART I — THE BRONZE AGE

Chapter II — CRETE

The story of Greece begins on Crete, a long, narrow island that lies midway between Europe (to which it belongs geographically), Africa and Asia. It separates the Aegean Sea (which laps against its northern coast) from the greater expanses of the Mediterranean to the south. Crete extends 152 miles from east to west, but its widest part measures only 35 miles. It covers an area of a little over 3,000 square miles. On a map the island looks a bit like a great horned slug slowly creeping westward across a

fig 4. — **Crete**

blanket of blue.

Imposing mountains tower above Crete's wide coastal plains. Snow-capped Mt. Ida rises 8,000 feet at the center of the island. The climate in the lowland areas is similar to that of

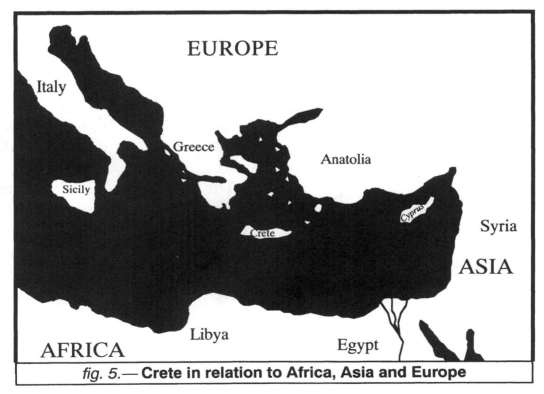

fig. 5.— **Crete in relation to Africa, Asia and Europe**

mainland Greece; hot and dry in the summer, and cool and wet in the winter. Although it rains frequently in the fall and winter, the showers don't last very long. Today, the island belongs politically to Greece.

Early Settlers

Crete is historically important because it was the first part of Europe to be civilized, and it had a substantial effect upon the development of Greek culture. The island's original settlers were probably mariners from Asia, who were blown off course as they ventured westward in their small, fragile crafts across the turbulent Mediterranean Sea. When they realized that they had stumbled upon an enchanting land of gentle breezes whose soil, although rocky, was quite fertile, they decided to remain. At first they lived in caves, but later they built huts of sticks and mud-bricks. Eventually their numbers grew as they were joined by others who landed on the shores of the pleasant island.

Neolithic Agriculture

The early settlement of Crete occurred around 4000 B.C., during the Neolithic period. *Neolithic* is a Greek word that means "New Stone Age." It followed a more primitive time called the *Paleolithic* period ("Old Stone Age"). These terms are used by archaeologists to define the era when human beings made most of their tools and weapons from the stones they found on the ground. It was during the Neolithic period that men first turned to agriculture to supply their food needs.

The first settlers of Crete grew barley and wheat, but later generations discovered that grapevines and olive trees flourished in the island's rocky soil and temperate climate. Wine and olive oil were to become important cash crops. They also herded sheep and goats for their wool and milk, raised pigs for their meat, and kept a few oxen to pull the plows that they had fashioned out of wood and stone. They even domesticated bees for honey to sweeten their food. (Sugar cane, our modern sweetener, originally grew only in New Guinea, an island in southeast Asia.)

The sea itself yielded a bountiful harvest of fish, which made up a substantial part of the islander's diet. They cut down cypress trees to build a fleet of broad beamed fishing vessels. They particularly savored the taste of octopus, which they speared just off the island's rocky shores and cooked in its own ink.

The Development of Trade

As the farmers prospered and the small villages grew into towns, some of the more enterprising islanders would load their boats with local produce and set sail for foreign trading ports. They brought back to Crete many new ideas and technologies as well as crafts and food products.

An early destination of these traders was the island of Cyprus which lay to the east. The people of Cyprus mined copper, a metal that could be melted down over a hot fire to make tools and weapons that were harder and sharper than the stone implements used on Crete. Once the merchant ships began bringing home supplies of the new material, Cretan craftsmen experimented with the process of melting it down and pouring it into molds. By 2500 B.C. they were producing fine copper daggers and spear points as well as kettles and other kitchen tools.

Trading vessels also sailed from Crete to Egypt, where the merchants exchanged wine, olive oil, timber, wool and copper tools for beautiful stone vases. The Cretan artists used the vases as models, but they later created their own designs of stone containers. Egypt was also the source of gold, ivory, precious stones, faience (a type of glazed clay), ostrich plumes and linen.

Perhaps the most useful Asian import was the potter's wheel. This simple mechanism consisted of a flat stone disc that revolved within a wooden framework. A craftsman placed a lump of wet clay on the disc; then, turning the disc with one hand, he molded the clay into a perfectly symmetrical bowl or jug.

A Superior New Ship Design

As the economy of Crete grew and flourished, more attention was given to the design of the vehicles of trade—the merchant ships. Storms in the Mediterranean can be quite violent, often occurring with very little warning, and so the Cretan shipbuilders created sturdy vessels that could endure the most blustery weather. Each ship had a very high prow that enabled it to cut through huge waves without swamping its decks, while its broad beam and deep keel made it extremely stable. These vessels were unquestionably the best afloat on the waters of the Mediterranean at that time.

The Cretan captains loved the challenge of the open sea, and their well-built ships became familiar sights at all the principal trading ports. They sailed to the Aegean islands to barter for obsidian, a black volcanic glass that could be carved into very sharp knife blades and spear points; it was also a favorite material for small statues. They sailed eastward to Syria where they obtained, among other objects, lapis lazuli, a beautiful blue stone used to adorn articles of jewelry. Around 2000 B.C. Syrian merchants introduced the Cretans to a new, man-made metal called bronze. It was formed by melting together copper and tin, and it was harder and sturdier than ordinary copper. This innovation marked the beginning of the Bronze Age in Crete. Some scholars believe that Cretan captains even ventured into the stormy Atlantic to obtain the necessary tin from the British Isles.

Pirates were always a menace in the ancient Mediterranean world. To protect their traders from attack by unfriendly parties, the Cretans built a fleet of swift armed ships. They patrolled the open seas and often escorted the merchant ships. This fleet was history's first navy.

A Powerful Kingdom

Over the centuries, Crete gradually evolved from a few coastal settlements to a vast network of over one hundred towns connected by paved roads. By 2000 B.C. there were three main cities on the island: Knossos, Phaestos and Mallia. Each was ruled by a king, who lived in a large palace overlooking the simple mud-brick houses of his subjects.

The civilization of Crete reached its

fig. 6 — **Major cities of ancient Crete**

peak of development around 1600 B.C. when King Minos of Knossos extended his rule over the entire island. His magnificent many-storied palace served not only as his home but also as a center for craftsmen, scribes, merchants and government officials. Some scholars believe that Phaestos and Mallia became the summer residences of Minos.

By this time, Cretan trade colonies had been established overseas in Libya, the Aegean islands, and Anatolia. By monopolizing the prosperous trade routes of the Mediterranean Sea, Crete had become one of the richest empires in the ancient world. Yet, when this great civilization came to an end in 1450 B.C. (we will find out what happened later in this chapter), it would be forgotten for thousands of years.

The Legend of the Minotaur

Until the end of the nineteenth century A.D., all that was known about ancient Crete came from the myths and legends created by the Greeks, who visited the island in the final years of its glory. The most famous of these stories concerned the Minotaur, a monster that was half-man and half-bull. This ferocious beast supposedly lived in an underground labyrinth or maze beneath the palace of King Minos. In Greek the word *Minotaur* means "bull of Minos."

According to the legend, King Aegeus of the Greek city of Athens killed a son of Minos in a battle that was ultimately won by the Cretans. To avenge his son's death, Minos ordered the Athenians to send a tribute of fourteen young men and maidens to Crete every nine years. (In some versions of the story it is an annual tribute.) These poor souls were locked in the labyrinth and preyed upon by the ravenous Minotaur. One year Theseus, a son of Aegeus, begged his father to send him along with the other youths on the terrible journey to Crete. The prince was determined to destroy the monster and end the sacrifices. Aegeus protested vehemently, but at last he granted his son's wish.

fig. 7 — **The Minotaur**

When Theseus arrived on the island of Crete, he was befriended by Ariadne, the beautiful daughter of Minos. She, of course, fell instantly in love with the handsome young Athenian, and she offered him a magical ball of twine that would guide him in and out of the labyrinth. In return for her aid, Theseus was to marry the fair maiden. The bargain was made, and the prince boldly entered the labyrinth, letting the twine slowly unwind until at last he caught sight of the dreaded Minotaur. A fierce battle ensued, but Theseus triumphed, slaying the creature with a bronze dagger. His mission accomplished, he swiftly retraced his steps through the labyrinth by recoiling the twine until he arrived at the entrance where Ariadne eagerly awaited him. He wasted no time and raced with her to a waiting ship. Athens no longer had to pay the terrible tribute.

The Meaning of the Legend

Legends, no matter how fanciful, are nearly always based upon actual historical events. As storytellers repeatedly describe the great feats of local heroes, they inevitably add embellishments and exaggerations to heighten the drama of the tale. For example, an account of the rescue of a drowning child by an old man can, as it is told again and again, easily evolve into a romantic story about a beautiful princess who is saved by a hideous monster!

If this is so, what could have been the basis of the legend of the Minotaur? We know from the records of Greek writers, who lived long after the fall of Cretan civilization, that at one time Athens was controlled by the island and forced to pay tribute. Perhaps the legend of Theseus and the Minotaur grew out of a successful attempt by the Athenians to throw off the "monstrous" yoke of Cretan authority and end the tribute.

Enter Sir Arthur Evans

But there was no physical evidence that the kingdom of King Minos had ever existed, and nearly everyone considered the ruler of Crete to be a mythical figure. Toward the end of the last century, however, Sir Arthur Evans dramatically changed our perception of Crete's place in the ancient world.

Evans was a wealthy British scholar who was forced by poor health to spend much of his time in the warm climate of the Mediterranean. One day, as he was poking about in an antiquities shop in Athens, the owner showed him some small engraved stones that had been found on Crete. The stones were covered with strange, squiggly markings that appeared to Evans to be a form of ancient writing. He was intrigued, and he immediately wondered about the possibility of deciphering the markings.

He needed more samples of the curiously engraved stones, and so he sailed to Crete. Upon his arrival there he set out to explore the island villages. Imagine his excitement when he discovered that many of the peasant women who were nursing babies wore stones around their necks that were similar to the ones he had obtained in Athens. The women called the objects "milk stones" and considered them good luck charms. They refused to part with them for any price, fearing that to do so would stop their production of milk, thereby causing their babies to starve.

Somewhat exasperated by his inability to obtain the milk stones, Evans decided to look for any similarly engraved objects that might still be buried in the ground. With this goal in mind, he bought some land in the small city of Knossos where a number of ancient artifacts had already been uncovered. It seemed like a promising site. In 1894 he hired a group of local laborers and began to excavate a large mound of earth and pebbles. What he found was much more than he had bargained for!

A Great Discovery

After uncovering several bits of broken pottery, a workman's shovel suddenly struck a substantial block of stone. At first Evans thought he might have stumbled upon the outer wall of an ancient city, but further digging revealed that he had found something even more significant. The block of stone turned out to be a part of a huge and sprawling building. As his men slowly uncovered the ancient ruins it occurred to Evans that this might be the legendary palace of King Minos! It was a gigantic structure covering nearly six acres and containing hundreds of rooms.

Evans spent the next six years excavating not simply a building but rather the remains of a great civilization, one that had been nearly forgotten for thousands of years. He named the culture Minoan after the famous king, and we will refer to it in that way from here on. Evans devoted the rest of his life to examining and restoring the historic palace, and in doing so he learned much about the lives of the people who had lived there in ancient times. He spared no expense, and the total cost of his efforts was over

$2 million! Fortunately, he was a very wealthy man.

The Palace of King Minos

The palace of Knossos is an extensive multi-level complex of rooms, corridors, and sweeping staircases. Constructed of blocks of gypsum (a local grey stone that contains unique configurations of crystals), the palace radiates from a central courtyard that is 200 feet long and 85 feet wide. Facing on the courtyard are a series of rooms that were used for official business; one contains an alabaster throne upon which King Minos himself might have sat (it is the oldest throne ever found). A wide stone staircase that once connected several floors of the building was originally lined with painted columns.

Light originally entered the palace through open shafts running from the roof to the ground floor. These are called light wells, and they are often used in modern buildings. Staircases and corridors led from the light wells to rooms on each level of the palace.

The Wonders of Minoan Engineering

Evans was amazed to discover that the Minoans had modern plumbing! A system of jointed clay pipes linked the palace with a mountain stream six miles away. Each pipe segment was tapered at one end in order to fit into the next piece. Stone bridges lifted the pipeline over gulleys and ravines so that the water could flow at a steady, slightly downward angle to the palace. These are the earliest known aqueducts. The system of pipes enabled the royal family to take showers and baths, and there was even a toilet that flushed when water was poured into it from a strategically placed clay pot!

The heavy rainfall in the autumn and winter months required adequate drainage in the roofs of the palace, and so the Minoan architects built an intricate system of ducts, gutters and basins on the outer walls to funnel the run-off. Some of this water was stored in tanks for drinking purposes or diverted into the plumbing system.

fig. 8 — **A section of the palace**

A Jumble of Rooms and Corridors

The design of the palace at Knossos is very asymmetrical (unbalanced). The rooms are of different sizes and shapes with hallways jutting off in all directions, and many interior walls are made up of multiple doors that could be opened to change the shape of a room. It seems that the original building was added on to in a piece-meal fashion whenever the need arose. Indeed, the entire palace seems to be a confusing, sprawling maze of rooms and corridors. Evans thought about this, and he wondered whether the legendary labyrinth of the Minotaur was actually the palace itself.

fig. 9 — **Diagram of the palace**

Works of Art Provide Clues to the Minoan Culture

Within the palace itself lay buried a great wealth of artistic treasures. The gold and silver jewelry, handsome stone statues and brightly painted pottery that have been unearthed reveal that the Minoans were superior craftsmen, and they also suggest that the upper classes lived in refined luxury.

The inner walls are decorated with beautiful frescoes that tell us much about everyday life on the island. Frescoes are pictures painted directly on wet plaster; as the plaster dries, the colors are absorbed and preserved within the wall surface. The Minoan artists had to work with speed before the plaster dried, and as a result their pictures seem spontaneous and full of life. Many of the paintings depict creatures of the sea: Dolphins, octopi and starfish swim across blue seascapes within borders of lotus blossoms, lilies, and olive sprays. The Minoan artists expressed a light-hearted enjoyment of nature, and they often took such playful liberties in their work as painting a rose blossom an unnatural green color or drawing a plant growing upside down!

Imaginary animals appear in many of the frescoes. The wall of the throne room is decorated with two griffins (mythical creatures that have the heads of eagles and the bodies of lions). The griffin was probably a symbol of the king's royal authority.

fig. 10 — **A griffin**

Of particular interest to Evans was a fresco that portrays a group of tall young men with slim waists and curled black hair wearing blue and gold loincloths. Each man carries a tall conical vessel. The figures seemed strangely familiar, and then he suddenly remembered seeing paintings of similar slim-waisted youths on the walls of Egyptian tombs that had been built around 1550 B.C. The Egyptians had called these figures *Keftiu,* which means the "Island People" from across the Great Green Sea (their term for the Mediterranean). Archaeologists had been puzzling for years over the identity of these men whose physical appearance differed so strikingly from that of the Egyptians. Now Evans had solved another mystery—the Keftiu were Minoan traders! Fragments of faience and metal objects from the Nile Valley that were buried amid the palace

ruins offered proof of trade relations between Egypt and Crete. Fortunately, the Egyptians had a custom of carving the name of the reigning pharaoh upon every valuable piece of art that they made, and this helped Evans to date the artifacts.

fig. 11 — **Keftiu**

Another fresco depicts three young acrobats engaging in an unusual sport, bull-vaulting. According to the painting, a Minoan acrobat would face a charging bull and, at the crucial moment, grab the animal's horns and then somersault onto its back. With a second somersault he catapulted from the beast into the waiting arms of one of his partners. Obviously such a feat was extremely dangerous, but what was its purpose? Was the bull-vaulting simply a form of entertainment, or did it have a deeper significance? And why was the bull so important to the people of

*fig. 12 — **Bull vaulting***

Crete? Evans thought hard and long about these questions.

Other palace wall paintings show young Minoan women with elaborately styled hair that is adorned with ribbons; they are wearing tight-waisted, flounced dresses and beautiful golden jewelry. Apparently an hour-glass figure was considered the ideal for Minoan men and women alike!

The Meaning of the Labyrinth

In one room Evans found a large bronze double ax, similar to axes that had been painted on the palace walls. It is likely that the double ax was another symbol of the Minoan king's authority. The Greek word for double ax is *labrys*, and so *labyrinth* means "the house of the double ax." Evans reasoned that visitors from mainland Greece must have been amazed by the great size and the sprawling design of the labyrinth. Undoubtedly they took stories back to Greece about the confusing maze of rooms and corridors that seemed to extend into infinity. If

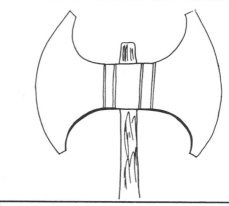

*fig. 13 — **A double ax***

this was so, then Evans was surely correct in his suspicion that the legendary labyrinth was in fact the palace itself!

Further Clues Suggest the Power of Knossos

The excavations at Knossos revealed that the sprawling palace was rather like a self-contained village, for it contained numerous workshops and storage areas in addition to the royal living and entertainment rooms and the government conference halls. Evans' discovery of large basement vaults that were once overflowing with gold, silver, and lapis lazuli was a further testament to the great wealth of the Minoan kings. The people of Crete paid their taxes in olive oil, and huge earthenware jars (called *pithoi*) designed to contain that useful liquid were found in storage rooms of the lower levels of the palace. Some of these jars are as tall as a grown man.

But despite the opulence of the Minoans, Evans found no sign of walls surrounding the palace. Apparently, the king's fleet of warships provided all the protection that was necessary! The Minoans must have felt very safe indeed in their island paradise, and this sense of security enabled them to channel their energies into creative activities rather than defensive or destructive ones.

Other sites on Crete have been excavated since the time of Evans, and archaeologists have found the ruins of many ancient cities and palaces. However, all evidence suggests that Knossos was the center of political and economic power during the height of the Minoan civilization.

The Religion of the Minoans

The Minoans worshiped many deities, but their religion seems to have centered upon one goddess. Carved statues of a female figure holding two snakes in her hands have been uncovered at many sites. In early times the snake was the symbol of regeneration; this is because as the snake grows it sheds its skin and emerges from it with a new set of scales. The snake goddess was probably worshiped as a source of fertility. The Minoans even kept tame snakes in their houses.

Religious ceremonies in Crete were most likely held in the open air, since few temples have been found on the island. Altars were built in palace courtyards and in sacred groves on hillsides and mountain tops. Offerings of food, double axes and statues of the

fig. 14 — **Snake Goddess**
Gift of Mrs. W. Scott Fitz — Courtesy, Museum of Fine Arts, Boston

clay figurines of female goddesses that were placed beside the remains of the deceased.

The Significance of the Bulls

Surrounding the Minoan religious altars and sanctuaries were stone walls crowned with chiseled bulls' horns. Even the palace had fragments of carved stone horns on the roof, and statues of bulls have turned up in excavation sites throughout the island. Minoan traders used solid gold weights in the form of bulls' heads to determine the prices of their wares. The design of the double ax itself contains two sets of bull horns, one the mirror image of the other. (See figure 16)

But why was the bull so important to the Minoans? The geography of Crete offers one answer. The island lies in a geographical area where earthquakes frequently occur. Indeed, the palace of Knossos was

gods were placed on the altars. The services were probably conducted by priestesses. The Minoans must have believed in an afterlife, because archaeologists have unearthed tombs containing spears, cooking utensils, and

fig. 15 — **Chiseled bull's horns**

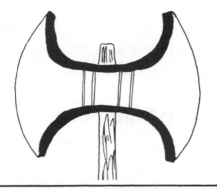

fig. 16 — Double ax with "horns" darkened

destroyed twice by earthquakes between 1900 and 1450 B.C. and rebuilt each time; the second time the Minoan workers reinforced the walls with wooden timbers to make them more flexible. Sir Arthur Evans was awakened one night by the sounds and movement of an earthquake. He immediately wondered whether the Minoans had thought they heard the muffled roar of a bull when the earth trembled. Primitive people often made sacrifices to creatures that they feared in the hopes of appeasing them. It is likely that the Minoans created their cult of the bull for a similar reason. They worshiped the image of the bull and made sacrifices to its spirit in order to spare themselves the terrible destruction caused by an earthquake. Perhaps even the bull-vaulting depicted in the palace frescoes was a ritual to appease the bull. Did the acrobats symbolize the Minoan people being tossed about on the back of an angry giant bull?

And what about the legend of the Minotaur? It is possible that on ceremonial occasions the king, as high priest of the land, wore a bull mask. The converging images of the sprawling labyrinth and the bull-headed man might very well have inspired the story of the monster living in a maze.

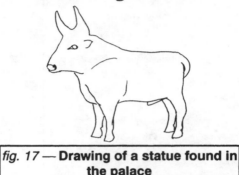

fig. 17 — Drawing of a statue found in the palace

Discovery of the Minoan Writing

We learned earlier that Evans originally began excavating at Knossos in order to find fragments marked with ancient writing. Fate was with him in this search, and he uncovered many clay tablets engraved with squiggly marks similar to those he had seen on the milk stones. As he studied the tablets, he noticed that they contained more than one kind of writing. The oldest ones contained primitive picture writing, such as a drawing of a fish, bird, or plant. Other tablets bore a more advanced kind of writing, a type of script.

To further complicate matters, there were two distinct kinds of script, which Evans named Linear A and Linear B. He worked for years trying to decipher the markings, but he was unsuccessful. In 1952, long after Evans had died, an architect named Michael Ventris deciphered the Linear B writing. Ventris was particularly excited to discover that the writing was an ancient form of Greek. Similar writing was also found on the mainland of Greece in Mycenae, a city we shall learn about in the next chapter. Perhaps Ventris could have eventually decoded the Linear A writing as well, but unfortunately he was killed in a car crash when he was only thirty-four. His death was a great loss for historians.

The Destruction of a Civilization

In 1450 B.C. the rich Minoan civilization came to an abrupt end. Sixty miles north of Crete lay the island of Santorini (called Thera by the Greeks). One day, a violent earthquake on that island set off a volcanic eruption that blew nearly everything to bits and sent a gigantic tidal wave 130 feet high racing toward the shores of Crete. Hundreds of thousands of Minoans who lived on the eastern part of the island drowned. The ports were destroyed and the once invincible royal fleet was badly damaged. And there was more to come. Over three feet of volcanic ash gently settled over the eastern regions of the island, covering everything—cities, villages, and fields—with a soft, highly toxic blanket. Those who escaped the forces of nature fled to the western hills, where they became simple farmers. The mighty power of the kings of Knossos was no more.

Questions:

1. Describe the geography of Crete.
2. Why is Crete historically important?
3. What were the early products of Crete?
4. How do you make bronze?
5. How did Ariadne help Theseus?
6. Why did Sir Arthur Evans go to Crete?
7. Describe the palace at Knossos.
8. What is the Greek meaning of labyrinth?
9. Why did the Minoans probably worship bulls?
10. How did the Minoan civilization come to an end?

Ideas to Think About:

1. Recently a group of American cowboys studied the bull vaulting of Crete. They insist that the feat portrayed in the frescoes is physically impossible. First of all, they say that it is impossible to maintain one's balance while grabbing the horns of a charging bull. Secondly, it is difficult to grasp both horns because a charging bull carries its head tilted to one side. If bull vaulting is a physical impossibility, the Minoan paintings must be purely symbolic of the Minoans' desire to master their erratic natural environment ("to grab the bull by the horns").

2. A Greek scholar named Plato (more about him in a later chapter) wrote a story about an island named Atlantis that was populated by a prosperous and civilized society. One day, unexpectedly, the island sank into the sea. Historians have been arguing for years about the existence and location of Atlantis. Many believe that Santorini was the island Plato had in mind. The eruption in the fifteenth century B.C. was so violent that most of the island was blasted away, leaving only the crescent shaped island that exists today. (Plato had said that Atlantis was ring-shaped.)

In 1967 scientists found in the ashes of the remaining part of the island three-story houses that are 3500 years old. In the houses were jars filled with wine and olive oil, farm tools, and everyday implements. The walls of the houses were decorated with beautiful frescoes. The similarity between the findings here and those on Crete indicate that the houses were inhabited by Minoans. The island must have been a colony belonging to Crete. And so, whether Santorini was Atlantis or not, the island provides invaluable clues to the civilization that flourished in Crete just before the eruption of the volcano.

3. Bulls play a major role in many Greek legends about Crete. In one, Zeus (the major god of the Greeks) disguises himself as a powerful white bull and charms a beautiful young maiden named Europa. As the girl climbs onto his back, he takes to the air and together they fly to Crete. There

fig. 18 — **Drawing of a Minoan bull's head found in an excavation in Greece**

Europa bears their son, Minos. The child grows up to become the famous king of the island.

4. Archaeologists have been aided in their efforts to establish the dates of Minoan artifacts by comparing them with similar objects made in Crete that have been found in the tombs of ancient Egypt. As we have learned (see page 18), the Egyptians wrote the name of the reigning pharaoh on their valuable works of art as well as upon the walls of their tombs and temples. Egyptian time periods were based upon how long the pharaoh had ruled, so that "Rameses 21" would be the twenty-first year of the reign of Rameses. This makes it very easy to date Egyptian objects, and archaeologists can assume that Cretan artifacts buried with them were made at about the same time.

5. Some scholars believe that Minos was not the name of one specific man. Rather, it was the term given to every ruler of Knossos, like the words *king* or *pharaoh*.

6. The first person to dig up ancient artifacts near Knossos (in 1878) was a Cretan merchant named *Minos* Kalokairinos! Could he have been a descendant of the legendary king?

Projects:

1. Theseus did not honor his promise to Ariadne. Find out what happened after the couple left Crete, and write a short report. Also, see if you can discover what happened to Aegeus when his son returned to Athens.

2. According to legend, the famous labyrinth was built for Minos by a Greek named Daedalus. Find out more about Daedalus, and discover how he and his son Icarus tried to escape from Crete. Draw a picture of their daring getaway.

3. After Sir Arthur Evans had excavated the palace at Knossos, he hired a group of artists, architects and archaeologists to help him restore certain parts of the structure to appear as they had in 1450 B.C. Great care was taken to make the restorations as authentic as possible, but many people feel that Evans should have left the remains of the palace as he found them. What do you think? Write a short report offering your opinion, giving reasons to back it up.

4. Make your own fresco painting. Mix plaster of Paris and scoop it onto a metal cookie sheet. Use a plastic knife to make a smooth, flat surface. When it is firm, but still damp, paint a design or picture. You must work quickly before the surface dries!

5. Many English words are derived from Greek. We learned that Neolithic means new (neo) stone (lithic). Can you think of three other English words that contain "neo"? Consult a dictio-nary. What do they mean? Use each in a sentence.

6. Bulls are also common symbols in modern cultures. For example, an active stock market is described as "bullish". Can you think of any other common expressions that refer to bulls? Do you know of a sports team called "the Bulls"? What characteristics does the bull symbolize? Make a poster illustrating the use of bulls in our culture.

Chapter III — THE EARLY KINGDOMS

Around the year 2000 B.C. horsemen from central Europe began moving southward onto the Greek peninsula. They were called the Achaeans by the Greek poet Homer, although modern scholars believe that the Achaeans were but one of many groups that invaded Greece over a period of several centuries. These warriors destroyed the small villages of the primitive people who were already living there and claimed the territory for themselves. They spoke a language that was a forerunner of Greek.

The Establishment of Self-Sufficient Communities

Each tribal chieftain seized the most arable land he could find and established a small kingdom there. On the highest promontory of his domain he built a walled fortress (called a citadel) where he and his family lived along with the soldiers and craftsmen of his clan. Most kingdoms were established on the eastern Peloponnese not far from the sea.

The common people built houses of wood and mud-bricks at the foot of the citadel and grew their crops in the surrounding area. They had to work hard to cultivate the thin, rocky soil. In fact, only one fifth of the land in Greece can be farmed at all because of the mountainous terrain. Yet, these primitive tribesmen succeeded in producing adequate supplies of wheat and barley to sustain their communities.

Grapes grew abundantly during the hot, dry summer and were gathered in the fall. They were placed in wooden vats and trampled by the families of the farmers until all the juice drained out. The crimson liquid was then poured into clay pots, where it fermented into a full-bodied wine, the preferred beverage of the higher ranking people.

Groves of gnarled, broad-trunked olive trees bore large quantities of fruit. The olives were gathered and pressed to extract an oil that had many uses. The early Greeks cooked with it and spread it like butter on their bread; they burned it in clay lamps for lighting and used it as soap when they scraped themselves clean; they offered it in ritual ceremonies to their gods and sent jars of it to the citadel as payment for their taxes. They later learned to mix it with honey to produce a solution that took the stiffness out of cloth!

The sheep and goats that contentedly nibbled the clumps of grass growing on the hillsides provided the early settlers with wool and milk. Powerful oxen pulled the farmers' plows. Horses were highly valued, and they were trained to draw war chariots. Using a horse for ordinary farmwork would have been unthinkable!

Craftsmen produced tools and weapons for the entire community. Like the Minoans, the Greeks learned to melt copper and tin together over a hot fire to produce bronze. Tools and weapons fashioned from this orange-colored metal were significantly harder and more functional than the primitive bone, flint and copper implements they replaced.

The chieftains came to be regarded as kings, and they passed on their power to their sons. When problems arose that affected the entire community, the king met with the heads of the leading families to discuss possible solutions. These advisors were the nobility of the kingdom.

The Beginnings of Trade

The Greeks supplemented their diet of grain with seafood, for the Mediterranean, as we have learned, was teeming with all sorts of tasty fish. At first, the fishermen ventured cautiously into the waters of the Aegean with nets ready and spears poised. Occasionally on such outings, the mountain peak of an offshore island would come into view. Actually, the Aegean islands are made up of the peaks of a submerged mountain range, and they are so numerous that a mariner sailing among them is never more than forty miles from some piece of land. Later generations of Greeks would settle on these scenic islands.

The sea opened up new possibilities for trade as well as fishing for the early Greeks. Sailing a small wooden craft was infinitely easier than trudging over high mountains, and the development of a local sea trade greatly increased communication among the kingdoms lying nearest the coast. At the same time, exploration of the calm waters of the Aegean inevitably aroused the Greeks' curiosity about what lay beyond the horizon.

A Common Bond

Although the pockets of civilization scattered across the mountainous peninsula remained strongly independent, the early Greeks were culturally bound together by a common language, a similar life style and a shared set of religious beliefs (and, of course, by trade). The ancient religion was based on the worship of many gods. The most important deity was the sky god Zeus, but Poseidon (god of the sea) and Dionysus (god of vegetation) were also greatly revered. The original inhabitants of the region had worshiped a female deity similar to the Minoan snake goddess, and she was incorporated into the evolving Greek religion.

A Warlike People

But in spite of the cultural bonds and the trade relations that had developed, fighting among neighboring kingdoms was fairly common. The early Greeks were fundamentally a warlike race, and disputes over land ownership often led to bloodshed.

fig. 19 — **The major kingdoms of early Greece**

Whenever an unfriendly army appeared on the horizon, the local farmers rushed inside the citadel walls for protection, and the warriors drove their chariots out through the city gates to battle the intruders.

The Super-kingdoms

By 1700 B.C. southern Greece was dominated by several powerful kingdoms: Tiryns, Argos, Thebes, Pylos, Athens and Mycenae. The smaller communities were reluctant to dispute the authority of these giants, and they came to depend upon their superior might in times of war. When invaders threatened an area, the leaders of the smaller kingdoms simply appealed to their stronger neighbors to defend the local territory. As a result, a kingdom like Thebes actually controlled a very extensive region.

By around 1600 B.C. Mycenae had become the most powerful kingdom in Greece, dominating the Peloponnese as well as several offshore islands where small Greek colonies had been founded. The Myceneans established a vast commercial empire and created the first great civilization of mainland Europe. They ruled for about five hundred years, and this period is known as the Mycenean Age.

Questions:

1. What is a citadel?
2. What were the uses of olive oil?
3. What factors bound all the Greeks together?
4. Who was Zeus?
5. Where was the Mycenean Empire?
6. What are the approximate dates of the Mycenean Age?

Ideas to Think About:

1. One reason for Mycenae's power was its prime location. The citadel overlooked a vast plain that stretched eastward to the sea. It was also close to the isthmus of Corinth (the narrow strip of land connecting the Peloponnese to northern Greece). This gave the Myceneans control of a major trade route. Any merchants wishing to enter or leave the Peloponnese had to travel through a pass near the foot of the Mycenean citadel, where they were obliged to pay a duty tax to the local officials for the privilege of continuing on their journey. The control of such strategic locations would play an important role in the power and prosperity of Mycenae for centuries.

2. Because the early Greeks made their tools and weapons out of bronze, the

period of ancient Greek history dating from 3400 until 1140 is called the Bronze age. It ended when iron was introduced into Greece.

Projects:

1. The early Greeks established a system of government in their kingdoms known to us as feudalism. The king and his nobles controlled the army, and the farmers were required to pay a tribute (a tax) in the form of grain in exchange for protection against invaders. In many ways, the early citadels resembled the manors and castles of the Middle Ages. Find out more about feudalism and write a short essay.

2. We have learned that the Aegean islands are actually the tops of submerged mountains (many are volcanoes). Find out how the Mediterranean Sea was formed and when the mountains of the Aegean were submerged in water. Write a short report.

3. Design a menu for the evening meal of a typical chieftain and his family. Think about what foods were available, and try to imagine how they would have been prepared. Be creative in your description of the various dishes. Examples: octopus simmered in wine sauce and olives stuffed with goat cheese. Don't forget dessert and beverages!

Chapter IV — THE MYCENEAN AGE

The Influence of Crete

As we know, the Minoans were skilled and experienced sailors who ruled the seas from about 2000 until 1450 B.C. During the early Mycenean Age the Minoan civilization was at its peak, and Crete controlled all the major trade routes and ports in the Mediterranean world.

The Myceneans had much to learn from the more sophisticated Minoans. Greek traders who sailed to the island brought back beautiful examples of Minoan craftsmanship. Mycenean artisans at first copied the imported objects, but they soon created their own styles and designs of gold and bronze jewelry, armor, molded bowls and cups, and decorative sword and dagger handles. Since the Myceneans were an aggressive, warlike people, their art lacked the delicacy and whimsy of the gentler Minoans. Yet, the metal objects produced by the Greek craftsmen were vastly superior in quality to those of most other Bronze Age cultures of the Mediterranean world.

Trade With Other Cultures

Mycenean merchant ships carried cargoes of olive oil, wine, sheepskins, timber, pottery and metal crafts to be traded for a wide variety of products in the ports of the eastern Mediterranean. These overseas business transactions made the Mycenean kings very wealthy. At the same time, Greek pirates further enriched the treasuries of their home cities by looting foreign vessels. The kings used this ill-gotten booty to pay their soldiers and to surround themselves with luxurious items in order to maintain an appearance of power and prestige.

The End of the Minoan Civilization

Do you remember how the civilization of Crete was destroyed by the volcanic eruption on the island of Thera? When the Myceneans discovered that most of the Minoan fleet had sunk and thousands of Minoans had drowned, they saw their chance to gain control of the Mediterranean trade routes. Wasting little time, they landed at Crete and made the island a part of their own expanding empire. They later rebuilt the damaged palace at Knossos and occupied that city for fifty years.

Discoveries of Early Greek Writing

Before all this happened, the Minoans had introduced the Mycenean traders to the concept of writing. The Greeks adapted the Minoan writing (called Linear A by Evans) to record their own language, thereby creating a new type of writing (Linear B). This is the writing that was decoded by Michael Ventris (see pg. 23). The Mycenean conquest of Crete explains why Linear B writing was found on that island beside examples of Linear A.

In 1939 archaeologists digging at the Mycenean city of Pylos on the Greek mainland found over one thousand clay tablets containing Linear B writing. It was similar to the writing found at Knossos by Evans. The tablets turned out to be inventory lists of articles stored in a palace: "one pair of wheels bound with silver, one pair of wheels bound with bronze (unfit for use)," and so on. Also included was a list of about one hundred early professions (such as potter, herdsman, and shipbuilder). This data has proved extremely useful for our understanding of the organization of Mycenean society.

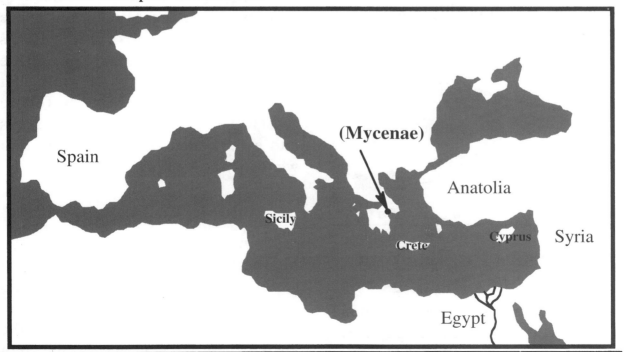

fig. 20 — **Mycenean trading centers**

Mycenae Rules the Waves

With the conquest of Crete, the Myceneans gained command of a vast network of trading stations from Sicily (an island off the southwest coast of Italy) to Syria. They established a colony on the island of Cyprus in order to obtain a monopoly over the local copper supply, and they sailed to Spain for tin, the other metal required for making bronze.

The Mycenean ships were slim yet extremely seaworthy; they were propelled by as many as fifty oars. Linen sails were hoisted on thick wooden masts to catch the wind. A large eye was brightly painted on the bow of each ship. This was probably a symbol of good luck.

fig. 21 — **Eye on the prow of a boat**

Mycenae Profits From Egypt's Decline

At the time that the Myceneans assumed control of Crete, Egypt was still a great power in the eastern Mediterranean. This highly centralized ancient empire extended from northeastern Africa to Palestine and Syria in western Asia, and Egyptian armies controlled most overland trade routes. After 1400 B.C., however, Egypt's power began to decline as its government grew weak and fragmented, and accordingly Mycenean pirates stepped up attacks on Egyptian ships.

The Need For New Markets

One hundred years later, Egyptian trade had slackened dramatically, and pirates had become such a constant threat to merchant vessels that few trading ports remained open. Seeking new markets, the Myceneans were drawn to the newly expanding towns that bordered the Black Sea. These towns had great stores of grain that were harvested on the very fertile coastal plains, and the local merchants had established trading centers that were already bustling.

A Strategic Site

A narrow strait leads from the Mediterranean into the Black Sea; it separates Europe from Asia. This channel of water was called the Hellespont (the modern name is the Dardanelles). The entrance to the strait

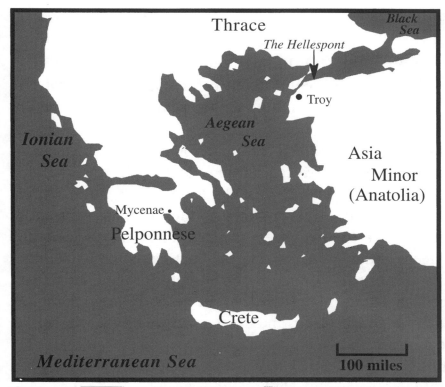

fig. 22 — **Troy overlooks the Hellespont**

in enriching the coffers of the Trojans by paying them tolls, and they relished the idea of commanding the strait themselves. The temptation to extend their power eventually proved irresistible, and so in about 1200 B.C. the Myceneans attacked and destroyed the city of Troy. This won them control of all the trade in the eastern Mediterranean as well as the Black Sea. It was an impressive victory, but it was to be their last.

was an important strategic site, because whoever built a city there could control the Black Sea trade and become rich by charging fees for those ships that passed through the strait.

Troy

In the twelfth century B.C. the city of Troy (the Greeks called it Ilium) occupied the highly prized location bordering the strait. Troy was built on a bluff on the Asian side of the Hellespont (in modern Turkey) high above the coastal plain that bordered the sea. The Myceneans had no interest

Questions:

1. What did the Myceneans learn from the Minoans?
2. How did the Mycenean kings feel about piracy?
3. Why did the Myceneans take over the island of Crete?
4. How did Mycenae become so wealthy?
5. What are Linear A and Linear B writing?
6. Why did the Mycenean traders look for new markets?

7. Why was Troy's location a strategic one?

8. What caused the Trojan War (the war between Mycenae and Troy)?

Ideas to Think About:

1. There is a famous Greek legend about Jason and the Golden Fleece. Jason was an adventurer who sailed his ship, the Argo, into distant waters to recover a magical golden fleece. Many scholars believe that the legend is based on the voyages of the Mycenean sailors who explored the shores of the Black Sea and brought home to Greece the gold they had obtained through trade. Others suggest that the golden fleece refers to the grain that was carried back to Greece.

2. The Myceneans used huge rocks to build the walls of their citadels. They carefully piled them in tiers without using mortar. Centuries later, the Greeks couldn't imagine how human beings ever could have lifted the massive rocks, and so they imagined that immortal giants called Cyclops constructed the (Cyclopean) walls. We will learn more about these huge creatures in a later chapter.

Projects:

1. Read the story of Jason and the Golden Fleece and present a short report about it for your class. What do you think the fleece represents?

2. Pretend that you are the captain of a Mycenean ship. How would you navigate your vessel? Remember, such basic instruments as the compass have not yet been invented, there are no accurate maps, and the boat has to be hauled up on the beach at night for the crew to eat and sleep. Write an entry in your ship's log, and draw a picture of your vessel.

3. The word Hellespont means "the Sea of Helle." Find out who Helle was and write a short report. Your best reference source is a book on Greek mythology.

4. Study the illustrations of Mycenean warriors in the books in your classroom. Then draw a picture of a Mycenean dressed for battle.

Chapter V — THE DORIANS

The Decline of Mycenae

By the middle of the twelfth century B.C., Mycenean civilization was in a state of decline. The constant warfare among the kingdoms weakened the strength and will of the people. Furthermore, despite the conquest of Troy, trade was not as lucrative as it had been in the days of the Minoans.

At the same time, the Myceneans were becoming increasingly alarmed by the growing numbers of uncivilized warriors who appeared on the northern borders of Greece. This ominous presence forced the Mycenean kings to focus their energies upon defense, and they began to strengthen the walls of the citadels and to stock up on weapons and food supplies. But they were not fully prepared for the destructive invasion that took place.

The Dorian Invasion

In about 1140 B.C. the Dorians, a race of horsemen even more ferocious than the Achaeans had been, swept down the Greek peninsula. They burst into the great citadels, looting or destroying everything in sight and killing the Mycenean rulers. They enslaved those people who did not manage to escape.

The Dorians were invincible because they had weapons made of iron. Indeed, their crudely wrought swords and daggers were considerably stronger than the handsome bronze arms of the Greeks. Furthermore, the Dorians fought with a savage brutality that startled even the Mycenean soldiers. Some of the Greeks managed to flee to the mountains of Arcadia in the central Peloponnese, where they eventually settled and clung to the ways of the past. Others fled to Anatolia and established colonies there. Athens somehow escaped the onslaught of the Dorian invaders and became a haven for Mycenean refugees.

The Dark Ages of Ancient Greece

The Dorians were primitive, illiterate nomads. They had little interest in art and writing, and as a result of their conquest the written language died out completely in Greece. The invaders settled in the valleys and on the plains, particularly in the regions of Messenia, Laconia and Argolid in the Peloponnese, where they took over the fields previously farmed by the Myceneans. Since they were not seafarers, all overseas trade came to an abrupt end.

Fortunately, the Dorians adopted some of the traditions and religious beliefs of the Myceneans, and so that rich culture was not entirely snuffed out. To their credit, the Dorians did bring to Greece superior tools and weapons made of iron, and although in many parts of the peninsula craftsmen continued to mold implements out of bronze, the Dorian invasion marked Greece's entry into the Iron Age. But by and large, the years between 1100 and 800 B.C. were a time of economic poverty and intellectual backwardness, appropriately called the Dark Ages of ancient Greece.

Questions:

1. Why was Greece in decline just before the Dorian invasion?
2. Why were the Dorians able to defeat the Greeks?
3. Where did the Greeks who escaped the Dorians finally settle?
4. What contributions did the Dorians make to Greek culture?
5. What were the Dark Ages?

Ideas to Think About:

1. The Dorians helped to memorialize the civilization they meant to obliterate in one important way. The fires that burned the Greek towns baked the clay tablets containing Mycenean writing (Linear B) and thus preserved them for modern historians to decipher.

2. The Dorians considered Doris, a region in central Greece, their homeland. They later claimed that they were descended from Dorus, a son of a legendary figure named Hellen.

Projects:

1. The Dorians learned about iron from a society in the Near East called the Hittites. Find out who these people were and write a short report.

2. Imagine how worried the Myceneans must have been about the Dorians. Write a short play about events leading up to the invasion or about its aftermath. Perform the play with some friends for your classmates.

3. The Dorians spared Athens. Why do you think this happened? Write a paragraph explaining why you think Athens was spared.

Chapter VI — THE WORKS OF HOMER

The Storytellers

The rich civilization of the Mycenean warriors would have been completely forgotten were its memory not kept alive in the legends recited by generations of storytellers (called bards) who lived after the Dorian invasion. During the grim years of the Dark Ages, the Greeks loved to listen to tales of the military exploits of the Mycenean heroes as well as myths about the gods of Mt. Olympus. Townspeople would gather eagerly around a central hearth in the evening to hear an itinerant bard describe the dramatic events of the heroic age that preceded their own simpler times.

Recitation of the Stories

The legends were usually recited or chanted in verse to the accompaniment of a lyre, an ancient stringed instrument resembling a small harp. These story-poems are called epics (from the Greek *epos* meaning "tale"). Since many of them were too long to be entirely memorized (recitations could last for hours), the storyteller would simply remember the basic plot as well as key words and phrases, repeating some of them at specific intervals; he would then improvise the verses in between as he went along. For this reason, each version of an epic was unique, although key phrases occurred again and again in all of them.

*fig. 23 — **A bard***

History's First Great Poet

Around 750 B.C. a bard named Homer (born on the Aegean island of Chios) composed two long epics set in Mycenean times. Similar stories had been told for hundreds of years, but Homer refined them and created the definitive versions which other bards subsequently recited, as accurately as they could, until the words were finally written down. According to legend, Homer was blind.

Homer's works are considered the greatest poems in Greek literature, and

*fig. 24 — **Head of Homer —** H. L. Pierce Fund, Courtesy, Museum of Fine Arts, Boston*

they are still read and enjoyed today. They are of great historical value as well, for they provide us with a detailed record of life in ancient Greece as well as vivid descriptions of the proud Mycenean warriors. The gods and goddesses of Mt. Olympus appear in human form and play an active role in the stories; in fact, Homer's works became a sort of Bible of the Greek religion, as we shall see in a later chapter.

THE ILIAD

The first of the two epics is called THE ILIAD. Its 16,000 lines describe the final days of the war between Mycenae and Troy (the Greeks called it Ilium). Homer's story, more fanciful than the historical account we read about in the last chapter, attributes the cause of the Trojan War to the vanity of three Greek goddesses. The story begins when Paris, a young prince of Troy, is told to choose whom among them is most beautiful. When he selects the goddess of love and beauty, she rewards him with the love of the most beautiful woman in the world. Her name is Helen, but unfortunately she is already married to Menelaus, king of Sparta in the Peloponnese.

Paris visits Sparta, and when Menelaus is conveniently called away to a funeral in Crete, the prince whisks Helen off to Troy. Upon his return, Menelaus learns of the kidnapping and resolves to get Helen back. He turns for support to his brother Agamemnon, the king of Mycenae, and in a short time Menelaus, Agamemnon, and several other Greek kings set sail for Troy with their soldiers in a thousand ships.

The city of Troy is surrounded by a huge, impenetrable stone wall. The Greeks lay siege to the city, but they cannot get inside the wall for ten years. From time to time the Trojans send out their best warriors to engage in hand-to-hand combat with Greek opponents, but the city itself remains invulnerable.

THE ILIAD focuses upon the events that occur at the very end of the siege. Homer relates how in the tenth year of the war a terrible plague infects the Greek camp. A soothsayer (someone who interprets the will of the gods and predicts the future) advises Agamemnon to release a woman captive (of whom he has grown fond) in order to end the plague. He releases the woman and replaces her with a slave girl belonging to another Greek king named Achilles.

Achilles is the greatest warrior in the Greek army, and he is very temperamental. Upon hearing what Agamemnon has done, he retires to his tent, where he sulks and refuses to fight the Trojans. At this inopportune moment Hector, another Trojan prince and the greatest of the Trojan warriors, suddenly appears outside his city's gates challenging Achilles to combat. But the petulant king refuses the challenge, and he sends his best friend Patroclos to fight in his stead. Although he struggles valiantly, Patroclus is no match for Hector, and he is ultimately slain by him. The terrible news of the death of his friend finally draws Achilles from his tent. He chases Hector three times around the walls of Troy, and when at last the two men face each other in combat, Achilles kills the Trojan prince. The battle scene between the two heroes marks the climax of THE ILIAD. The epic ends rather

fig. 25.— **Achilles and Ajax playing draughts during the siege of Troy**
H. L. Pierce Fund, Courtesy, Museum of Fine Arts, Boston

abruptly after King Priam of Troy begs for the return of his son's body for proper burial and Achilles honors the request.

THE ILIAD is a rich resource of information about the weapons and military strategies of the Mycenean Age, and it reveals much about the character of the warriors themselves. For them, personal honor and courage were the highest of the manly virtues. Indeed, Achilles' greatest wish is to achieve glory: to die nobly on the field of battle and to be remembered by future generations for his valor. (His wish is later granted.) Homer was an unbiased man, and in his epic enemy warriors appear to be as heroic as the Greeks.

fig. 26 — **Sack of Troy — from a classical Greek vase —** *Courtesy, Museum of Fine Arts, Boston*

THE ODYSSEY

The fall of Troy is described in Homer's second epic, THE ODYSSEY, a lively and exciting adventure story. It begins when Odysseus, the king of the Greek island of Ithaca, devises a plan to end the long siege. Following his orders, the Greeks build a huge wooden horse, place it outside the Trojan city gates, and then pretend to sail home. The Trojans, believing the horse to be a peace offering, open their gates and drag it inside. Unknown to them, inside the belly of the horse are several armed Greek soldiers, led by Odysseus himself. There is, of course, much feasting and celebrating in Troy. That night, while the Trojans are slumbering, the Greeks climb out of the horse and open the gates of the city for their comrades (who have sailed back). The Greeks destroy the city, kill most of the Trojans, and free Helen. She returns to Menelaus (who forgives her for everything!).

Nearly half of THE ODYSSEY describes the many obstacles that Odysseus encounters on his voyage home, a voyage that should have required only a few weeks but instead takes ten long years. Homer's graphic descriptions of Odysseus' formidable adversaries, including the one-eyed Cyclops, the man-eating Laestrygonians, the lovely enchantress Circe (who turns men into pigs!), the bird-like Sirens (whose song no man can resist), and the many-headed Scylla enliven an action-packed story that is hard to put down. Nor do Odysseus' troubles end with his arrival home, for he then has to deal with the persistent suitors of his faithful wife Penelope who have turned his palace into a hotbed of decadence.

Odysseus embodies the character traits the Greeks most respected: intelligence, cunning, and resourcefulness. Against seemingly impossible odds, he uses his wits to outsmart his opponents and regain his kingdom. And yet,

*fig. 27 — **The wooden horse***

Odysseus is not perfect, for he cannot resist the opportunity to boast of his achievements. This, in fact, is the cause of his difficulties, the reason for his treacherous and drawn-out voyage home. The Greeks considered excessive pride (they called it *hubris*) among the worst of human weaknesses. We shall learn more about the pitfalls brought about by pride in a later chapter.

Problems of Historical Accuracy

Although Homer's two great epics appear to describe life during the Mycenean age, it is important to remember that the poet lived hundreds of years after the fall of Troy. For this reason, many of his descriptions actually apply to his own times while others reflect his impression of what life might have been like in the earlier age. THE ILIAD and THE ODYSSEY thus provide an invaluable wealth of information about both the Mycenean Age and the Dark Ages. The challenge to us is to decide which descriptions belong to which period!

Until fairly recently, scholars thought that Homer's stories concerned imaginary happenings in imaginary places. They considered the two epics outstanding pieces of literature, but no one contemplated the possibility that they might be based upon historical fact.

Questions:

1. How were the early epics recited?
2. What are the names of Homer's two great works?
3. According to Homer, what caused the Trojan War?
4. What was Achilles' greatest wish?
5. What does THE ILIAD tell us about the character of the Mycenean warriors?
6. What was Odysseus' clever plan to end the siege?
7. How long did it take Odysseus to return home?
8. Describe Odysseus' personality.
9. Are Homer's works historically accurate?

Ideas to Think About:

1. In THE ODYSSEY Homer describes a beautiful island named Phaeacia where the people love dancing, hot baths, and comfortable beds. The men are skillful sailors and merchants. Scholars believe that Homer was thinking of Crete when he wrote about this island paradise.

2. The works of Homer were known in Africa as well as Europe. Earlier in this century, over six hundred ancient papyrus texts were discovered in Egypt that contained parts of the famous Greek epics.

3. It took the ancient bards a long time to recite an epic; they usually covered one section each evening. To get an idea of how long an entire recitation took, consider the case of a sixty-year-old man who recently recited a poem the length of THE ODYSSEY. Reading aloud for two hours in the morning and another two hours in the afternoon, he required two weeks to complete the work!

Projects:

1. "Beware of Greeks bearing gifts" is an expression frequently used in modern everyday conversation. What is the derivation of this expression and what does it mean? Write a short paragraph that describes an example or two that illustrate the truth of this expression. (Marc Aronson, a student at Fay School, suggests that "Beware of gifts bearing Greeks" is an equally valid warning!)

2. Read as much as you can of a modern version of THE ILIAD or THE ODYSSEY. There are many simplified versions available.

3. Iphigenia was the daughter of King Agamemnon. Her story is told in the short book A FAIR WIND FOR TROY by Doris Gates. Read the book and write a short report.

4. Today an "Achilles' heel" refers to a vulnerable spot. Look up the story of Achilles and find out why his heel was vulnerable. How was his vulnerability used against him in the Trojan War?

5. Do you accept Achilles' ideal of living a short but glorious life rather than a long, uneventful one? Why, or why not? Write a paragraph explaining your point of view.

6. What is the meaning of the expression, "her face launched one thousand ships?"

7. Originally the word "odyssey" simply meant the story of Odysseus. What does it mean today? Consult a good dictionary. Use the word in three sentences, and make it a part of your vocabulary.

8. Cassandra tried to warn the Trojans about the wooden horse. Consult a book on mythology and find out why the Trojans did not accept her advice.

Chapter VII — THE DISCOVERIES OF SCHLIEMANN

A Self-Made Man

Heinrich Schliemann was a German businessman who believed that the stories about Troy and Mycenae actually took place. As a child, he had listened with rapt attention as his father read to him passages from THE ILIAD and THE ODYSSEY, and from an early age he determined to find the places described so vividly in Homer's works. Schliemann had little money but a great deal of ambition. His formal schooling was minimal, but he read every book he could get his hands upon and became a self-educated man. He even taught himself eighteen languages!

Schliemann realized that his archaeological projects would be very expensive. He knew he had a good business sense, and so he became a trade merchant, traveling to many parts of the world in search of products that he could sell profitably. By his mid-forties he had amassed a small fortune, and he was able to devote the rest of his life to that which interested him most: the search for the sites described in Homer's epics.

In Search of Troy

He began his quest for Troy in 1870 at Hissarlik, a small Turkish town built above a broad plain and overlooking the Dardanelles. The local geography seemed to match Homer's description of the region surrounding the walled city of King Priam. Furthermore, a huge mound of earth protruded above the level area of the town, and Schliemann suspected that it might contain artifacts dating from the ancient past. Archaeologists call a mound of earth made up of the ruins of an early culture a tel.

A Systematic Approach

Schliemann hired over one hundred workmen to help him excavate the tel. He approached the digging in a systematic way, organizing the site into many small sections. He carefully recorded his findings so that the original configuration of soils, rocks and buried materials could be studied at a later time. This was a novel approach, because up until then most people digging for ancient artifacts were

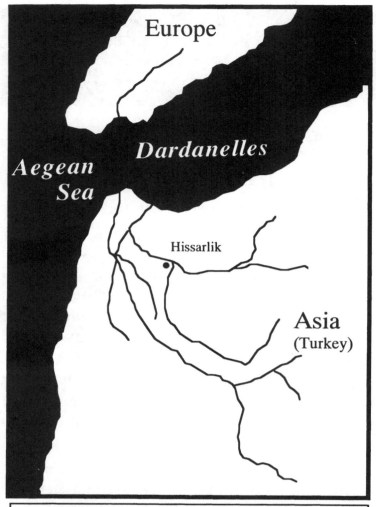

fig. 28 — Site of Troy in western Turkey

destroyed.

Schliemann's interest was not to become rich (he already was!) but rather to gain knowledge of lost civilizations. He established a procedure that, with many refinements, is followed by archaeologists to this day. For this reason, Schliemann is considered the Father of Scientific Excavation.

The Discovery of Multiple Troys

The tel at Hissarlik turned out to be the most complex archaeological site ever excavated until that time. As his workers cut through the layers of earth, Schliemann was astonished to see the remains of nine cities that had been built one on top of the other.

The reason for the layering of cities is simple. Like most peoples of the ancient Mediterranean world, the Trojans had built their homes of mud-bricks. When the walls of a house became old and unsturdy, they were simply knocked down, and a new house was built upon the same site. In the case of fire, earthquake or general destruction caused by war, an entire city might

basically treasure hunters; they shoveled aggressively in the soil, tossing aside any objects that were broken or made of inferior materials as they looked for priceless objects in "mint" condition. As a result, many fragments of ancient pottery, broken tools and weapons as well as the ruins of buildings were permanently lost or be reduced to rubble. If the site appealed to a later group of settlers, they would simply level off the area and build their houses over the ruins of the earlier city. Centuries of this process of building a city upon the site of an earlier one gradually resulted in the creation of a mound of earth made up of many layers. Each layer, then, represented one city, the oldest lying at the bottom and the most recent near the

fig 29 — The Nine Cities of Troy		
Troy	**IX**	c 300 BC - AD 400
	VIII	c 700 - 300 BC
	VII	c 1300 - 1100 BC (Homer's Troy)
	VI	c 1800 - 1300 BC
	V	c 1900 - 1800 BC
	IV	c 2000 - 1900 BC
	III	c 2200 - 2000 BC
	II	c 2500 - 2200 BC (site of Priam's treasure)
	I	c 3000 - 2500 BC

top. For a modern archaeologist, digging into a large tel is like slicing through a many-layered cake.

Which City Was Homer's Troy?

In the second layer Schliemann uncovered the ruins of fine houses and strong fortifications. He found an altar that had been used for sacrifices, a paved road and even the remains of a palace. When a workman chipping at the hardened sediment with his shovel suddenly struck something smooth and shiny, Schliemann was called to the spot. As he gently knocked away the pieces of rock, he realized that he was uncovering a cache of ancient artifacts. He was overjoyed, but he tried not to reveal his excitement. According to his written account, Schliemann told his workers to take off the rest of the day; they must have been delighted with the unexpected holiday, and their employer was now free to uncover the buried treasure in private. Once he was alone with his wife Sophie, he carefully uncovered a priceless collection of gold cups and vessels, silver vases, copper daggers, and gold jewelry. Over eight thousand priceless articles had laid buried in the earth for over three thousand years! He called these objects

"King Priam's Treasure." For Schliemann, they were proof that he had uncovered Homer's Troy!

fig. 30 — Objects included in Priam's Treasure

Recently, however, archaeologists using sophisticated scientific technology have concluded that it was the seventh city, and not the second, that Homer described in THE ILIAD. The objects found by Schliemann were buried hundreds of years before the Trojan War took place! Actually, the fact that they belonged to an earlier period makes their discovery even more important than Schliemann believed it to be. They are the works of craftsmen who lived long before the Greeks built their stone citadels on the Peloponnese.

Damage to Parts of the Site

Unfortunately, Schliemann's excavation methods were clumsy by modern standards. In an effort to make a cross section of the site, he dug a huge trench across a major part of the tel, shoveling away everything in his path. To make matters worse, his efforts to uncover the second city inevitably damaged a large portion of the ruins of buildings and walls that made up the more recent seventh city—the Homeric Troy that he was actually seeking! Fortunately, Schliemann's detailed journal of his findings contains some useful data about the materials that were shoveled from the trenches.

Schliemann Leaves Turkey

Schliemann had ordered his workers to take the rest of the day off because he wanted to keep his discoveries for himself. He felt no obligation to share "Priam's Treasure" with the Turkish government, and so he smuggled it to Germany. The Turks were furious when they found out what he had done, and they refused to let him dig in Hissarlik any longer. Schliemann offered to compromise by sending the Turks a huge check that was to cover the value of Priam's Treasure. But by this time he was ready to leave Turkey, confident that he had discovered Homer's Troy. His attention now turned to mainland Greece, and he sailed there in 1874.

A New Project

Just as Agamemnon had returned to his kingdom in Greece after the conclusion of the Trojan War, Schliemann made his way from Troy to Mycenae in hopes of discovering more clues about the heroic warriors described by Homer. There was no mystery about the location of the site of the Mycenean citadel, since the ancient walls had remained visible since the days of the Dorians. He employed 150 workers to dig there for him.

The Citadel at Mycenae

The structure of the wall itself was of great interest to Schliemann. Built of huge limestone blocks that fit snugly together, it was twenty-three feet thick and (in some places) sixty feet high. At about the time of the destruction of Knossos, a Mycenean king had rebuilt the hilltop palace buildings and reinforced the wall. Its sheer massiveness indicates how concerned the early Greeks were about war and the defense of their cities. When the Dorians became a dangerous threat in the twelfth century B.C., the wall of Mycenae was extended around an underground spring in order to insure a supply of fresh water during a state of siege.

The entrance gate to the citadel was capped with a magnificent stone relief sculpture of two (now headless) lions on either side of a tall column. Originally the lions had faces of colored stone or gilded bronze that were pegged into holes in the background stone slab. Their eyes, probably made of glistening gems, would have looked down majestically upon those who entered the citadel. The lion gate is one of the earliest coats-of-arms in history; the lions signify the power of the king as he defends his city (represented by the column).

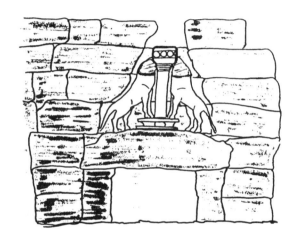

fig 31 — **The lion gate**

The Treasury of Atreus

Mycenae had been excavated by others before Schliemann arrived upon the scene. A huge tomb built in the shape of a beehive (called a tholos tomb) had been discovered outside the walls of the citadel. A tholos tomb was basically an earth-covered mound with a stone interior; a long entrance passage led to the conical chamber. The tomb's beehive shape was formed by rings of carefully cut stones, each ring slightly smaller than the one immediately below it. Tholos tombs had been built for the kings of Mycenae between 1500 and 1200 B.C. Similar structures that must have served as models for the Greeks have been found in Crete.

fig. 32 — A tholos tomb

The chamber of the tholos tomb at Mycenae was huge, measuring nearly fifty feet in width and height. It had originally been filled with gold and bronze objects; the body had been buried in a pit within the chamber. Schliemann visited the tomb when he arrived at Mycenae. He called it the Treasury of Atreus, because since ancient times it had been believed that Atreus, father of King Agamemnon, had been buried there. Although the contents had been plundered long ago, the structure of the tomb revealed the impressive architectural skill of the Mycenean builders. Furthermore, the vastness of the tomb suggested that the king who ordered it built possessed great wealth and power. Sadly enough,

at the time Schliemann visited the tomb it was being used as a sheepfold!

In Search of the Royal Graves

Schliemann's appetite for a dramatic discovery in Mycenae had been whetted by his success in Hissarlik. He reasoned that if he could locate the major tombs of the other Mycenean kings, he might find golden objects as extraordinary as those in Priam's Treasure. Since the tholos tomb and a few smaller graves had been found outside the city walls, scholars assumed that any other tombs would lie in the same vicinity. Schliemann, however, had other ideas. He knew the language of the classical Greeks, and he had read the diary of a Greek traveler named Pausanias who had visited Mycenae as a tourist 1600 years earlier. Pausanias had observed stone gravestones marking the tombs of Agamemnon and some of his followers, and he noted in his diary that these were located within high stone walls. And so while many people scoffed at his decision to dig within the walls of the citadel, insisting that he was looking in the wrong place, Schliemann broke the ground just inside the main gate.

An Exciting Discovery

His efforts were amply rewarded. Not far below the surface he found a round double fence of stone slabs, known to modern archaeologists as Grave Circle A; the fence encircled five upright gravestones. Excitedly, Schliemann dug beneath the gravestones and discovered five deep shafts that had been cut into the rock. These were the undisturbed tombs of a royal cemetery predating the graves found outside the walls! At the bottoms of the shafts lay nineteen skeletons, buried in rich garments lavishly decorated with gold. A small baby's skeleton was dressed in a complete suit of gold. Five of the men had beautiful golden death masks placed on their faces. They were the same type of mask that the ancient Egyptians placed upon the faces of their royal mummies.

Around the skeletons were scattered a vast number of valuable personal possessions such as gold bracelets, signets, diadems, drinking cups of gold and silver, vases, swords and daggers, mirrors, and golden breastplates. One of the cups so closely resembled the one belonging to King Nestor described in THE ODYSSEY that Schliemann immediately referred to it as "Nestor's cup."

Nothing like this had ever been found before in Greece. Those artifacts that had been recovered at other sites were of very different styles and dated from later periods. Schliemann was ecstatic. Homer had mentioned that Mycenae was "rich in gold," and these objects certainly proved that he was right! In fact, more gold was found in these shafts than in all the other Greek sites excavated up to the present time.

Just as he "knew" he had found Homer's Troy, Schliemann was convinced that he had found the tomb of the children of Atreus (Agamemnon and his siblings). As he lifted one of the golden masks to the light, he dramatically exclaimed, "I have looked upon the face of Agamemnon!" But once again he was mistaken, for the mask as well as the other articles in the graves had been buried four centuries before Agamemnon was born. Modern archaeologists, noting the Cretan influence in the elaborate handles of the daggers and in the lines of the cups and the jewelry, confirm that the graves date from early Minoan times.

fig. 33 — The "mask of Agamemnon"

The objects found in the Mycenean graves are of great historic value. Many of the golden cups and plates are decorated with scenes from daily life, and these are excellent records of the dress and activities of the early Myceneans. A bronze dagger is decorated with pictures of hunters carrying huge shields and battling lions. The graves also bear witness to the extensiveness of the Mycennean trade network, for they contain silver stags from Anatolia, ropes embossed with amber stones from the region of the Black Sea, and ostrich eggs from Nubia (the African kingdom south of Egypt).

Schliemann's inaccurate estimate of the dates of the Mycenean shaft graves does not lessen the importance of his discoveries. To the contrary, the ancient Greek culture probably changed very little during the few hundred years separating the craftsman who made the golden masks and the warriors who fought at Troy.

Later Discovery of Other Tholos Tombs

Other tholos tombs have been discovered since Schliemann's time. Many of these were used for multiple burials, and one has been found that contains twenty skeletons. Apparently, when an important person died, the tomb was reopened and the old bones were simply moved out of the way to make room for the new ones! Given their massive size, these tombs must have been built for the kings and their families. Who else could have afforded such grand final resting places? Nine tholos tombs have been discovered in Mycenae, while forty have been located at the sites of other Bronze Age cities. Some of the tombs still contained valuable objects, including a suit of bronze body armor and several metal helmets decorated with boars' tusks that closely resemble those described in THE ILIAD.

Other smaller gravesites called dromos tombs have also been discovered; more crudely constructed than the tholos tombs, the dromos tombs are basically long, narrow caves. Several hundreds of these smaller burial sites have been excavated in and around Mycenae. They probably once held the bodies of high-ranking warriors and their families.

The Palace

Since Schliemann's time, the remains of the buildings of the citadel have been carefully unearthed. They are grouped around a courtyard. The palace itself has a large hall (called a megaron) surrounded by wide stone pillars; in the center of the hall is a circular hearth. On the right, against the wall and facing the hearth, stands the king's throne. Similar megarons have been uncovered in other Mycenean citadels in Tiryns and Pylos. They strongly resemble the main room in Odysseus' palace described in THE ODYSSEY.

The walls of the Mycenean palace were once covered with bright frescoes, a further indication of Minoan influence. Among the paintings that have survived are scenes of battle and wild boar hunts. Some of the Greek warriors depicted are carrying shields shaped like figure eights similar to those Homer described in THE ILIAD. Figure eight shields were also painted upon the walls of the palace of Knossos at the time of the occupation of the island by the Myceneans.

fig. 34
Figure 8 shield

Later Years

Schliemann visited many parts of Greece and excavated extensively at the ancient citadel of Tiryns. Once again, he was guided by the writings of Pausanius. Toward the end of his life he traveled to Crete, where he hoped to purchase land in the vicinity of Knossos to look for clues to a civilization that he suspected was even older than Mycenae. (Remember, this was before the time of Evans.) He was unable to purchase the land, and so he reluctantly abandoned the project. He later regretted that he had not been more persistent, for he came to believe that Crete was the original site of the Mycenean civilization. As we have learned, his thesis was inaccurate. Yet, he had come closer than any other scholar to discovering the Aegean civilization that had flourished long before the fall of Troy. Sir Arthur Evans would soon carry on where Schliemann had left off.

Our Debt To Schliemann

We owe a great deal to Heinrich Schliemann. Before he made his dramatic discoveries at Troy and Mycenae, historians believed that Greek civilization began in about the sixth century B.C. We now know that the great achievements of the Greeks living in the fifth century B.C. had their roots in the cultures of the peoples who settled on the rocky peninsula nearly fifteen centuries earlier.

Schliemann's work also showed that Homer's descriptions of the early Greeks were fairly accurate. Of course, those ancient epics must be read with an understanding that they were written centuries after the fall of Mycenae.

Questions:

1. Why was Heinrich Schliemann considered a "self-made man?"
2. Why is Schliemann considered the Father of Scientific Excavation?"
3. Why were there so many Troys?
4. Describe Priam's Treasure.
5. What is a tholos tomb?
6. What is the lion gate?
7. Tell the story of the discovery of the golden "mask of Agamemnon".
8. What is a megaron?
9. Why did Schliemann want to dig in Crete?
10. Why is Schliemann so important?

Ideas to Think About

1. Large sedimentary rocks that have been sliced through by blasts of dynamite line the highways in many parts of our country. The lines on these rocks resemble the layers that Schliemann found in the mound in Hissarlik. Look for these rocks as you ride along a turnpike, and when you see one, imagine that each line represents an important stage in an ancient culture. (Actually, each line does represent a specific geological era.)

2. Although Heinrich Schliemann was a brilliant man, he was also a great romantic. As we have learned, he loved the works of Homer so much that he desperately wanted to believe that he had found objects dating from the times described by the famous bard. Toward the end of his life, he began to realize that he lacked sufficient evidence to prove the authenticity of Priam's Treasure and Agamemnon's mask, and some scholars were even questioning whether he had found Homer's Troy. Such miscalculations seldom occur today, because modern technology enables archaeologists to date ancient artifacts with great accuracy.

3. Schliemann was "mad" about ancient Greece. Before he began his excavation projects, he advertised in a newspaper for a Greek wife. At the age of forty-seven he chose a bride of nineteen from among the photos sent him. Fortunately, the marriage turned out well: Sophie adored her husband and considered him the most brilliant of men. She bore him two children, whom he named Andromache (the name of the wife of Hector) and Agamemnon (this is no surprise!). When the children were baptized, Schliemann laid a copy of THE ILIAD on their heads and recited one hundred verses aloud! He even

named his servant Pelops, and his house in Athens was called Bellerophon (another figure from Greek mythology).

4. It is important to remember that the artifacts discovered by archaeologists tell us but part of the history of an ancient people. Only the rich owned golden jewelry and bronze weapons, and only they were buried in stone tombs. The ordinary people wore jewelry made of flowers and were buried in the soil; not much is left of them or their possessions!

Projects:

1. Archaeologists are working in many regions of the United States. Find out if there is a historical archaeological site near you, and write a short report about it.

2. Unlike most ancient royal burial sites, the grave shafts at Mycenae were not robbed. Can you explain this? (Think about how deeply the shafts were dug) Write a report that justifies your opinion.

3. Sophie Schliemann was an interesting woman. Find out what you can about her and write a short report.

4. Priam's Treasure was kept in Berlin for many years. In 1945 it mysteriously disappeared, and it has only recently been recovered. What do you think happened to it and why? (Hint: this was during World War II) Write a short paper presenting your explanation for what happened.

5. Think about the cities of Troy the next time you have a slice of many-layered cake for dessert!

6. King Pelops (remember him?) established a famous dynasty at Mycenae. His most well-known descendants included Atreus, Agamemnon, Iphegenia, Orestes and Electra. But his family was doomed to suffer terribly because he once cheated in a chariot race. Find out more about the circumstances of the race. Then write a short play about what happened.

PART II — ATHENS ACHIEVES GREATNESS

Chapter VIII — THE RISE OF THE CITY-STATE

Greek Government After the Dorian Invasion

For several centuries after the Dorian invasion, the inhabitants of mainland Greece were mostly illiterate farmers who led simple lives. Yet, the sparks of ingenuity and creativity that had burst into flame during the Mycenean Age were never fully extinguished, and toward the end of the Dark Ages there was a gradual rekindling of intellectual activity. The period of Greek history from 750 to 500 B.C. is known as the Archaic Age. This was a transitional era, a time when the Greeks hesitatingly and awkwardly took the first steps in a process of self-discovery that would lead to an explosion of creative energy in the Golden Age of the fifth century.

Early in the Archaic Age, the Greek people lived in small, isolated villages. Each community was led by a leader who was called an *archon*, a Greek word meaning "ruler." Our word "monarch" (meaning "one ruler") comes from this ancient term. Like the kings of earlier times, the archon depended upon the support and advice of his best warriors. The amount of arable land was extremely limited in the small mountain valleys (the average valley was only twenty miles long and less than twelve miles wide), and so neighboring villages were constantly fighting with each other for possession of local territory. This, of course, was nothing new in Greek history.

The Villages Expand

At first many of the the villages were built on the sites of the old Mycenean citadels. But as the population of a village increased, new houses and workshops were built at the base of the hilltop. Eventually, everyone lived at the foot of the high ground, which then became the sacred setting of temples and religious shrines.

As the population of an area continued to expand, a town and the villages and farms surrounding it were organized into a community unit known as a city-state. The Greek word for city-state is *polis*. This ancient word is an important root in our vocabulary: "politician" and "police" are two modern English words derived from it, and there are many others. The word *acropolis* means "the high city" where the temples were built.

In Athens nine archons ruled together. They were chosen from the most powerful and influential men in the polis. This type of government is called an *oligarchy* ("rule by the few").

Another Greek word that is useful to know is *cratos* meaning "power." When the power of a community was in the hands of the social elite, it was called an "aristocracy" (which literally means "power of the best.") In modern times, the aristocrats are the "blue blood" families whose ancestors were powerful in the government and economy of a society.

A Review of Greek Terms

Our study of ancient Greek history will introduce us to many Greek words that frequently turn up in the English language. In figure 35 are some that we have encountered so far (notice how many of them have the same roots).

The Major Regions

Most city-states were relatively small, having an average population of five to ten thousand people. That is about the size of a small New England town. Only three expanded to encompass a large area of land; these were Sparta, which ruled over the region of Laconia (and later Messenia as well), Athens, the focal point of the triangular peninsula of Attica (an area of one thousand square miles), and Thebes, a city dominating the fertile region of Boeotia.

Elsewhere in Greece, the smaller city-states savored their isolation and remained proudly independent. In these close-knit communities all the inhabitants knew one another, and the central marketplace and temple were visited by everyone on a nearly daily basis. No wonder the local pride was strong!

polis	city-state
acropolis	high city (or height of the city)
police	someone who protects the people of the city
politician	someone who works in the government of the city
archon	ruler
monarchy	rule by one man
oligarchy	rule by a few
cratos	power
aristocracy	power by "the best"
democracy	power by the people

fig. 35 — **Some English words derived from Greek**

fig 36 — **The major regions**

Corinth was a polis whose strategic location on the narrow isthmus connecting the Peloponnese to the rest of Greece brought its people great wealth through trade. Ships bearing goods from the Aegean to the Ionian Sea and vice versa were hauled up on rollers at Corinth (later wagons were used) and pulled along a roadway across the isthmus to the Gulf of Corinth on the western shore. The Corinthians controlled this roadway (indeed, they had built it!), and they collected tolls from everyone who used it. Given this preoccupation with commerce and products, it is not surprising that Corinth was the only polis where craftsmen were held in higher esteem than soldiers.

Sparta, a Dorian Stronghold

Sparta was the most powerful city-state on the Peloponnese. When the Dorians first invaded the plains of Laconia and founded Sparta, they enslaved the local Mycenean farmers, whom they called Helots. The Helots were forced to work the land and produce food for their tyrannical overlords. This arrangement enabled the invaders to devote all of their time to military matters. However, the Spartan soldiers had to keep a watchful eye over the toiling Helots, who outnumbered them seven to one.

At first the Spartans traded with other Greeks and imported products from abroad. Their culture was as rich as that of other city-states. Spartan craftsmen molded fine metal objects and sculpted beautiful vases. Music was an important part of their religious festivals, and a bard living in Sparta named Alcman is believed to be the inventor of love poetry.

As the polis grew, the Spartans seized new land to create additional fields for growing grain. In 735 B.C. they conquered Messenia, a fertile region in the southwestern Peloponnese, enslaving the local inhabitants. A century later the Messenians revolted against their rulers, and this event caused a great transformation in the structure of the government and the political philosophy of Sparta. Because it took the Spartan soldiers seventeen long years to bring all the Helots under control, their leaders decided to take drastic steps to insure that such a thing would not happen again. Henceforth, Sparta would be a tight military state, ever on the alert for signs of civil unrest. All trade came to a halt as the community turned inward; the people became extremely conservative and avoided contact with the outside world. The protection of the Spartan way of life was considered more important than the rights of the individual, and the soldiers became the unquestioning servants of the central authorities.

In the sixth century B.C. the desire to dominate a larger territory led Sparta to create a confederation of city-states known as the Peloponnesian League (headed, of course, by the Spartans). Now every polis in the Peloponnese was either directly controlled by Sparta or committed to support Spartan interests in times of war.

The Growth of Athens

The city of Athens had been a refuge to many of the fleeing Myceneans at the time of the Dorian invasion. During the Archaic Age, the Athenians kept alive the memory of the accomplishments of the Mycenean Age, savoring the ancient myths and legends as well as Homer's marvelous epics. Although all Athenian men were expected to serve in the army, military matters never became the major preoccupation that they did in Sparta.

Surrounding Athens was the plain of Attica where farms produced large quantities of wheat, grapes and olives while sheep and goats grazed in the untilled areas. As the city expanded, the local farms could not produce enough

food to support the population. The Athenians dealt with this shortage by trading their local crafts for wheat produced in other city-states. Slowly a merchant class began to grow within the community, and Athens was on its way to becoming an important trading center.

Ionia

Ionia was a coastal region in western Anatolia (see figure 45). It had been colonized by Mycenean refugees fleeing from the Dorians in the early twelfth century B.C.

The Greeks settling in Ionia were generally tradesmen rather than farmers. They obtained large quantities of grain from the native people and shipped it back to Greece. Over the years, Ionia would become an international center where people from European, African and Asian cultures mingled to trade their products and exchange new ideas. The ancient city of Miletus was the most important Ionian seaport.

Lydia was a kingdom lying to the east of the Ionian colonies. It was the first ancient culture to mint money. The Ionian merchants quickly picked up the idea of using coins instead of bartering goods, and before long the practice spread to the Greek mainland.

The Creation of the Greek Alphabet

For centuries after the Linear writing of the Myceneans died out, the Greeks had no written language. This situation changed when the Ionians came into contact with the Phoenicians, a sea-faring people living on the coast of western Asia (modern Lebanon). The Phoenicians had developed an alphabet of symbols that stood for consonant sounds. Written in combination, these "letters" represented words (the vowel sounds had to be reasoned out and added by the reader). This was a significant improvement over the cumbersome picture writing (hieroglyphs) of the Egyptians.

The Greeks adapted the Phoenician alphabet to record the sounds of their own language, and they improved upon it by adding symbols for vowels. By 720 B.C. the 24-letter Greek alphabet was in common use in Ionia, and, like the concept of coinage, it quickly spread to the city-states of the mainland. Our alphabet is based upon the one devised by the Greeks in those early times.

The alphabet was easy to master, and it dramatically improved communication throughout the Greek world. Writing soon became an essential part

A	alpha	A
B	beta	B
Γ	gamma	G
Δ	delta	D
E	epsilon	E *(short)*
Z	zeta	Z
H	eta	E *(long)*
Θ	theta	Th
I	iota	I
K	kappa	K
Λ	lamda	L
M	mu	M
N	nu	N
Ξ	xi	X *KS*
O	omicron	O *(short)*
Π	pi	P
P	rho	R
Σ	sigma	S
T	tau	T
Y	upsilon	U
Φ	phi	Ph, F
X	khi	Kh, Ch
Ψ	psi	Ps
Ω	omega	O *(long)*

fig. 37 — **The Greek alphabet**

of everyday business transactions, and new ideas could be shared and circulated as never before. Furthermore, Homer's epic poems could be recorded for posterity. (Some scholars believe that the need to record Homer's works was the crucial factor that inspired the Greeks to develop a written language.)

A Written Code of Laws

Earlier in this chapter, we learned that Athens annually elected nine archons. These men chose among themselves a leader, who was called the *archon eponymos*. He was the most important man in the polis. In 621 B.C. this lofty position was occupied by a man named Draco, and he is known as the author of the first Greek written code of laws. The code represented an important step in the protection of the rights of the individual. Up until then, the Athenian leaders had resolved local disputes according to their personal whims; now they were obligated to follow an unwavering standard when deciding guilt and dealing out punishments. But Draco's laws were harsh indeed, requiring the death sentence for someone found guilty of stealing a cabbage! And farmers who went into debt were ordered thrown into prison. Today the word "draconian" refers to a rule or law that has harsh penalties.

Yet, the Greeks had come a long way. Although there had been other written legal codes in the ancient world (most notably Hammurabi's Code in Babylonia and the Mosaic laws of Israel), the Greek system was designed to improve the lot of the people, rather than simply that of the ruling class.

Solon's Revisions of the Laws

In 594 B.C. Solon, an archon considerably more humane than Draco, revised the Athenian code of laws. He declared that farmers who fell on hard times should no longer be imprisoned, and he removed the death penalty for all crimes except murder. He also set up courts with juries drawn from the ordinary people.

In an important reorganization of the government, Solon created the Council of Four Hundred (also called the *Boule*); this elected body of men selected archons and set the agenda of items to be discussed by a larger assembly of citizens called the *Ecclesia*. Any Athenian male who had a certain income could attend the meetings of the Ecclesia. The *Aeropagus*, a group of retired archons which was empowered to make new laws, was now opened up to members of the upper class who had not been archons.

By restructuring the government in this way, Solon established a framework for Athenian democracy. However, despite his efforts to involve more of the people in the political process, only affluent Athenians were eligible to attend the assembly meetings and to be elected to high office. Women, slaves (of whom there were a great many) and immigrants from other city-states had no say at all in the local government.

Solon revitalized the Athenian economy by encouraging the exportation of olive oil as well as jugs and vases of glazed pottery to overseas ports; these became the chief products of Attica for centuries to come, and Athens' flourishing economy stimulated trade in other parts of Greece as well.

Political restructuring was not limited to Athens. By the sixth century a majority of the Greek city-states had abandoned the old system of kingship in favor of a government led by a group of nobles (an aristocracy). The most notable exceptions were Sparta and the conservative farming region of Thessaly, both of which continued to cling to the past.

Later Political Developments in Athens

Not long after Solon's death in 559 B.C., Athens was ruled by a military commander named Peisistratus. Although he had seized power (he was, in fact, a tyrant), he did not change Solon's government reforms; rather, he further reduced the power of the upper class in favor of the common people. Nor were his interests limited to political matters. Homer's works had become an important part of the Greek cultural heritage by this time, and Peisistratus commissioned a group of writers to prepare a definitive text of THE ILIAD and THE ODYSSEY. But perhaps his greatest contribution was to build up a powerful fleet and a strong army to defend Athens against invasion. This military might would play a crucial role in the defense of the entire Greek way of life, as we will learn in a later chapter.

The make-up of the Athenian government continued to evolve under the guidance of an archon named Cleisthenes. He divided all of Attica into small areas called *demes* that followed the boundary lines of the property owned by long-established clans. Then he created ten electoral districts, each containing a cross-section of the demes (each district was thus made up of parts of several demes). This new political make-up prevented any one district from totally supporting the policies of a single clan leader. The citizens in each district voted for men to represent them in the Boule and at other official meetings.

Now all Athenian citizens had a voice in a government that was responsive to the needs of the entire polis, and for this reason Cleisthenes is considered the founder of Athenian democracy. However, the wealthy continued to hold the most important administrative offices, because they were the most educated and they had the most free time (they were the idle rich of ancient Athens!). The Aeropagus eventually became a much esteemed judicial body, a sort of Supreme Court.

Both Peisistratus and Cleisthenes welcomed immigrants from other parts of Greece, particularly poets and artists, and this greatly enriched the artistic development of Athens.

The Expansion of Greek Civilization

By the sixth century B.C. there were nearly 150 city-states of varying size in mainland Greece. Overseas colonies were flourishing not only on the Aegean islands and in Ionia but also on the shores of the Black Sea and along the coasts of Italy, France, Spain, and northern Africa (see figure 38).

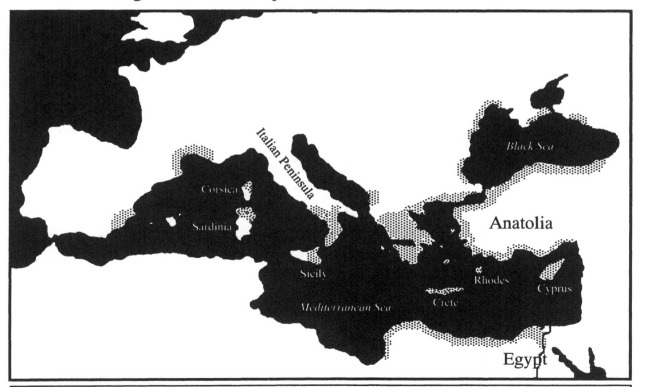

fig. 38 — **Greek colonies**

In mainland Greece, the geography of an area often influenced the lifestyles of the local population. For example, the people living in the cattle country of Boeotia became skillful merchants as they marketed their leather products. *Boeotia* literally means "cowplain"! The people of Corinth grew rich through trade; they were considered loud, brash and materialistic by other Greeks. Arcadia was a land-locked area, and its inhabitants were clannish and backwards. The farmers of Thessaly were hard-working and conservative. Ionia, a gathering place for people of many cultures, became a center for intellectuals. Athens prospered as its tradesmen brought home business profits as well as cargoes of grain from the overseas colonies; artisans from other parts of Greece flocked to the city that was rapidly becoming a center of creative activity.

A Common Culture

Despite the isolation and regional characteristics of the city-states and the land squabbles that frequently arose among them, the Greeks continued to share the bonds of a common language as well as long established religious traditions. They looked down upon the uncivilized tribes to the north whose utterances sounded to them like the mindless "bar bar" of sheep, and they referred to anyone who did not speak Greek as a "barbarian." Pride in their common heritage and love for their homeland nourished a sense of patriotism among the Greek people that was to prove an important advantage against foreign invaders.

Questions:

1. What is an archon?
2. What is an acropolis?
3. What city-state cared the most about military matters, and why did it do so?
4. How did Athens deal with the problem of a food shortage?
5. How did the Greeks improve upon the alphabet of the Phoenicians?
6. Why does "draconian" mean harsh?
7. How did Solon improve the Athenian government?
8. Why is Cleisthenes considered the founder of Athenian democracy?
9. What bonds held all Greeks together?
10. What is the derivation of the word "barbarian?"

Ideas To Think About

1. The ancient Greeks called themselves the Hellenes (the descendants of a legendary hero called Hellen). Today the Greeks call their country Hellas, and specific periods of Greek history are referred to as Hellenic and Hellenistic. Why, then, do we call them the Greeks? The name goes back to a colony in Italy founded by people coming from the Greek village of Graica. The colonists were called the Graii which was translated as *Graeci* in Latin, the language of the Romans. In English *Graeci* becomes "Greek". This term was applied to all people coming from Greece. To be accurate we should be speaking of the Hellenes, not the Greeks, but it is difficult to change a tradition carried on by historians for over two thousand years!

2. Peisistratus seized power in an ingenious way. He slashed his body with a knife and gashed the sides of the mules hitched to a wagon. Then he drove the mules into the Athenian marketplace and shouted that he had been attacked by political enemies. The assembly immediately voted to give him a bodyguard. He then used the guard to attack the city, crush the government, and declare himself ruler! On another occasion (in an effort to regain the power he had lost), he arranged to have a large woman dressed in gold armor driven in a chariot into Athens; claiming to be the goddess Athena, she said, "trust Peisistratus." The people accepted her advice, and he regained power!

3. A variety of sweet seedless grapes was grown on the hillsides of Corinth. They are the source of our modern "currants".

4. When a polis established a new colony, it (the polis) became the mother (*metro*) polis. This is the derivation of our word "metropolis," which means "the city and its surrounding suburbs" (the adjective is "metropolitan").

Projects:

1. Here is a game the class can play. Study the chart showing the Greek alphabet on page 66. Divide into two teams. Each team should have a copy of the Greek alphabet. The teacher writes a short message using the Greek letters and gives a copy to each team. The first team to translate the message wins. Now try another message.

2. It has been said that Draco's laws were written in blood, not ink. Explain what this means.

3. One out of every ten words in English come from the Greek language. We have learned about some that have to do with government (see page 62). Some other examples are amnesia, catastrophe, enigma, choir, chorus, agony, apology, school, orchestra, pentathlon, and thesis.

Below are some Greek words and prefixes and their meanings. See how many English words you can make by combining various Greek word roots and prefixes. (Examples: *bios* [life] + *graphein* [to write] = biography [written account of a life]; *hippos* [horse] + *potamos* [river] = hippopotamus) Can you think of other related English words?

anthropos	man	*moros*	foolish
archaeos	ancient	*pan*	all
auto	self	*para*	close, beside
biblion	book	*pathos*	feeling, emotion
bios	life	*philos*	loving, lover of
crypto	hidden	*phone*	voice
cyclos	wheel	*physis*	nature
dromos	racecourse or arena	*poly*	many
graphein	to write	*potamos*	river
hemi	half	*psyche*	mind, soul
hex	six	*rhinos*	nose
hippos	horse	*sophia*	knowledge or wisdom
logos	word	*sphere*	a round object
mega	great	*tele*	far
micro	small	*thermo*	warm
mimos	imitation	*tri*	three
mono	single	*zelos*	ardent feeling

Chapter IX — THE GREEK RELIGION

Why the Myths Were Created

The early Greeks did not understand the natural phenomena that occurred around them every day, and so they attributed such happenings as a sudden clap of thunder and the endlessly changing tides of the sea to the powers of divine spirits. From the days of the Achaeans every town and village had its own local deities, such as the god of the eastern meadow and the goddess of the mountain stream. There were, in fact, hundreds of Greek deities, each one controlling some aspect of nature. The early people also thought deeply about their own species; they wondered why humans suffered and why they died—and what happened to them after they ceased to breath? They concluded that their own destinies must also be controlled by invisible spirits.

Over the years the more imaginative thinkers created a collection of stories (called myths) about the activities of the unseen beings that seemed to rule the natural world. These myths provided fanciful explanations for how the world got to be the way it was. Every generation contributed new stories as more questions were asked. Eventually there evolved a hierarchy of gods and goddesses—most of them with human-like form—who were believed to be responsible for the creation and the functioning of the universe. This mythology formed the core of the Greek religion. The people readily accepted the sensational tales about the gods, and for a long time their belief in the powers of these deities made them less anxious about the forces of nature. If they could not control a bolt of lightning, at least they could understand why it existed.

Of course, there were some people who questioned the role of the gods and sought other explanations for natural phenomena; we shall learn about the discoveries of these early scientists in a later chapter. For now, let us focus upon the colorful deities who formed the nucleus of the early Greek religion.

The Myths Are Recorded

The myths were passed down from generation to generation by word of mouth until the advent of writing. Homer was the first to actually describe the physical appearance and personalities of the gods and goddesses, and his epics are filled with lively episodes in which the deities intercede in the lives of the human characters. Hesiod was a Boeotian poet of the eighth century B.C. who was profoundly influenced by Homer. He wrote a long religious poem entitled THEOGONY that drew together many of the circulating myths of his time, presented the genealogies of the gods (their family tree), and offered the Greek version of the creation of the earth. Most writers who came later used the works of Homer and Hesiod as their primary sources, and in time every educated man was able to quote long passages from them by heart. A common knowledge of the mythology spiritually united all the people living in the widely scattered city-states of Greece.

Beginnings

The Greeks believed that before there was a world as we know it, there was only confusion (Chaos). Out of Chaos sprang Mother Earth (Gaea) and the sky (Uranus). A huge, tempestuous sea (Ocean) encircled Gaea. Applying this information to their rather sparse knowledge of geography, the ancient Greeks reasoned that southern Europe, western Asia and northern Africa (which they considered a part of Asia) made up the land areas of the earth, and that this land was surrounded by a vast and infinite body of water. Gaea's name can be seen in the words *geology* and *geography*, sciences related to the makeup of the earth's surface.

After Gaea had created all the plants, Uranus provided them with life-giving rain. The water filled the lakes and rivers. Then Gaea and Uranus created the animals, as well as all sorts of nymphs, fauns, and other nature spirits.

The Next Generation

The children of Gaea and Uranus were called the Titans. There were twelve of them, including Hyperion (the sun god) and Phoebe (goddess of the moon). The most powerful Titan was Cronus. Gaea and Uranus also produced some terrible monsters called the Cyclops, huge one-eyed creatures (their name means "wheel-eyed").

Later, Gaea was greatly angered when Uranus cast the ugly Cyclops down to the dark Underworld. Seeking revenge for this crime against her offspring, she persuaded Cronus to attack his father with her sharp flint sickle. When he did so, drops of the blood of the wounded sky god turned into fearsome-looking Giants (they would be enemies of the later gods) and the three bat-winged Eumenides (the avengers of the unpunished sins of men). You might know the Eumenides by their Roman name, the Furies. Uranus was then banished by his son; but before departing, he predicted that some day Cronus, too, would be deposed by one of his own children.

Cronus Becomes King

Following the departure of Uranus, Cronus became the king of the Titans, and his sister Rhea became his wife. But Cronus could not forget his father's terrible prophecy. In a determined effort to protect his reign, he snatched up each of the five babies that Rhea bore him and swallowed it. Rhea was horrified, and when she became pregnant for the sixth time, she secretly went to Mount Lycaeum in central Greece to bear her child. After the birth Cronus asked to see the baby. Rhea cleverly wrapped a stone in some blankets and presented it to her husband; believing that the bundle was his child, Cronus promptly swallowed the stone. As

for the baby (a boy named Zeus), he was taken to Mt. Ida in Crete to be raised by nymphs and a magical goat named Amaltheia who fed him through her horns.

Zeus Assumes Power

Zeus grew into splendid manhood, and his mother dreamed of the day he would become king. Since Cronus had never seen his son, it was easy for Rhea to introduce Zeus into the divine court

fig. 39 — **Head of Zeus**
Theodora Wilbour Fund No. 1, Courtesy, Museum of Fine Arts, Boston

as a royal cup-bearer; this position enabled him to prepare a noxious potion and to serve it to Cronus in his golden cup. The drink made the king violently ill, and he spat out all five of the children he had swallowed: the goddesses Hestia, Demeter and Hera and the gods Poseidon and Hades. Since they were supernatural beings, they were quite unharmed (and fully grown).

Then Zeus and his brothers (Poseidon and Hades) attacked their father and drove him off. Uranus' terrible prophecy had come true! Afterwards, the brothers liberated the Cyclops from the Underworld; in gratitude for their freedom these rather hideous creatures made thunderbolts for Zeus, a forked trident for Poseidon, and a magical helmet for Hades that would render him invisible. The thunderbolts helped Zeus to subdue the other Titans and thereby rise to the pinnacle of divine power.

The Kingdom Is Divided

The three brothers divided up Cronus's kingdom: Poseidon became the god of the sea, Hades (also known as Pluto) was to rule the Underworld (the land of the dead), and Zeus assumed command of the heavens as well as supreme authority over all the gods and goddesses. Demeter became the goddess of the harvest, Hestia the goddess of the hearth, and Hera the goddess of women and of childbirth.

The Olympians

Zeus and his siblings resided in a beautiful palace on Mt. Olympus. This is the tallest mountain in Greece, rising nearly ten thousand feet into the heavens near the coast of Thessaly. Its snow-capped, cloud-covered peak create an aura of mystery, and for the early Greeks it seemed the perfect dwelling place for their gods.

Zeus had many children, born to his wife (and sister) Hera as well as to his numerous other loves. The most important were Apollo (the god of music, health, and prophecy), Artemis (goddess of the hunt), Ares (the god of war), and Hephaestus (the god of metal working). Athena (goddess of wisdom and of combat) was born to Zeus' first wife Metis in a most unusual way. Having heard a prophecy that any child of his born to Metis would become greater than himself (any self-respecting king considered himself the greatest of all!), Zeus changed the pregnant Metis into a fly and promptly swallowed her. But he soon developed a terrible headache, and he begged Hephaestus to split his skull open with an anvil in order to lessen the pressure

fig. 40 — **Birth of Athena — Painting on an ancient vase**
H. L Pierce Fund, Courtesy Museum of Fine Arts, Boston)

(a gruesome act, but remember, gods don't die!). Zeus's suffering ended abruptly when Athena sprang fully grown and fully armed from his head. He had nothing to fear from this child, since she was born to *him* and not Metis! Another Olympian was Aphrodite, the goddess of love, who simply burst into life from the foam of the sea (*aphros* is the Greek word for foam). Some myths suggest that she sprang to life from the blood of Uranus.

Altogether there were twelve major gods and goddesses (ruled by Zeus) who supposedly lived in a majestic bronze-floored palace on Mt. Olympus. On the next page is a list of their names, functions, and special symbols.

The Olympians

ZEUS, god of the heavens and king of all the gods; his symbol was the thunderbolt; also sacred to him were the eagle and the oak tree.

HERA, wife of Zeus and protectress of wives and mothers; her symbols were the pomegranate, the cow and the peacock.

POSEIDON, god of the sea; his symbols were the trident, the dolphin and the horse (he gave the first horse to man).

ATHENA, goddess of wisdom, reason and purity, protectress of civilized life; a warrior, she was Zeus's favorite child (she carried her father's breastplate called the aegis); her symbols were the owl and the olive tree.

DEMETER, goddess of the harvest and of fertility; her symbol was the sheaf of wheat.

HESTIA, guardian of the hearth

APOLLO, god of music, light, health and prophecy, he was the son of Zeus and Leta; his symbols were the lyre and the laurel tree.

ARTEMIS, goddess of the hunt (and twin sister of Apollo); her symbols were the cypress tree, the moon, the deer, and the hunting dog.

APHRODITE, goddess of love and beauty; her symbols were the rose, the myrtle tree, the dove, the sparrow, and the dolphin.

ARES, god of war; a bloodthirsty fellow, his symbol was the vulture.

HERMES, Zeus's messenger and god of thieves, business and mischief; the son of Zeus and Maia, he was cunning and shrewd; he wore a winged hat and winged sandals and carried a cadeusus (a staff entwined with two olive branches—later two snakes—and capped with a set of wings). Today the cadeusus is the symbol of medicine.

HEPHAESTUS, god of metalworking and smiths, and patron of crafts; his symbol was a hammer.

HADES (Pluto), god of the Underworld. An important god, although he did not live on Mt. Olympus.

DIONYSUS, god of wine; his symbol was a cluster of grapes. He later replaced Hestia on Mount Olympus.

fig. 41 — **Apollo and Artemis**
Catharine Page Perkins Fund, Courtesy Museum of Fine Arts, Boston

The Olympians Mirror Society

The ancient Greeks imagined that the family of Olympic gods resembled those of their own leaders. Since in earliest times they were ruled by kings, they envisioned Zeus as a powerful monarch. And just as the king and his family and noblemen originally lived in a citadel on an acropolis high above the houses and fields of the ordinary people, so too Zeus lived in a beautiful palace atop the highest mountain in Greece.

Greek society is reflected by the Olympians in other ways as well. For example, Greek leaders often enjoyed the company of more than one woman; Zeus had several wives as well as numerous affairs. Greek women did not have the freedom to do anything about their husbands' activities, and Hera was continually angered and frustrated by Zeus's carryings-on.

Nearly all the Olympic gods were very handsome and the goddesses were beautiful. The exception was Hephaestus, who was ugly and lame. Ironically, Homer tells us that he was married to Aphrodite, the goddess of love and beauty. A magic fluid called ichor flowed through the veins of the deities, and they dined on nectar and ambrosia (this divine food and drink made them immortal). Yet, the gods were far from perfect beings, as we have seen with Zeus; they often exhibited such unpleasant human weaknesses as pride, envy, and even dishonesty.

The Gods Play An Active Role In Human Events

Life could be dull on Mt. Olympus, and so the gods often amused themselves by manipulating the everyday lives of the mortal humans who lived on the earth below. They could disguise themselves as practically anything—an old beggar, a young child, or even a bird—and suddenly appear among ordinary people. Sometimes they even fell in love with human beings and had children with them, thus producing offspring that were half-human and half-god (such half-breeds were not immortal).

Believing that the universe was controlled by the gods, the Greeks reasoned that a deity would help a human who pleased him (or her) or inflict pain and suffering upon someone who angered him. Thus convinced that their very lives were in the hands of the gods, the Greeks worshiped the Olympians constantly, offering prayers to the appropriate deities before they did anything important. For example, they prayed to Poseidon for a safe sea voyage, to Ares for success in battle, to Demeter for a good harvest, and to Dionysus for a full-bodied wine. When something went wrong, they assumed that one of the gods had been offended, and they hastened to offer an effusive prayer begging forgiveness.

The Greeks even sacrificed animals to please the gods. After a sacrificial goat or ox was slaughtered, its entrails (internal organs) were often removed and examined by priests who specialized in this procedure. The Greeks were very superstitious, and they believed that such natural maladies as a bloated goat liver predicted bad times for the community, while a bright color detected in newly retrieved intestines

fig. 42 — **Head of Aphrodite**
Francis Bartlett Donation of 1900, Courtesy Museum of Fine Arts, Boston

was a good omen! Once the organs had been examined, the slaughtered animal was roasted over a fire. The thigh bones were wrapped in fat and burned as an offering to the god, but the rest was eagerly consumed by the worshipers. Actually, religious ceremonies were among the few occasions when meat was eaten by the Greeks, whose typical meal consisted of bread, fruit, vegetables and cheese. We will learn more about their diet in Chapter XIV.

Local Traditions

Every city worshiped its own patron deity and local gods in addition to the Olympians, and altars were set up in homes and public places. Food and wine were traditionally offered to the neighborhood spirits at every meal. Annual festivals held to honor the patron gods provided the people with an opportunity for merry-making and feasting after the conclusion of traditional processions and sacrifices. In these local festivals lay the origins of Greek theater and the Olympic Games, which we will study in depth in later chapters.

Every town had a public hearth dedicated to the goddess Hestia. When a city-state founded a new colony, it sent fire from its official hearth to ignite a new hearth in the colony. This tradition symbolized the kinship between the old and new communities. The fire was probably transported via a large smoldering log that was packed in hot coals and placed in a metal container. In the same spirit of kinship, a new bride always carried a burning log from her family hearth to light the fire in her new home.

Religion As a Civic Activity

The religion that evolved in Greece was closely tied to the daily lives of the people, and its mythology as well as its rituals and ceremonies created a rich heritage. Yet, there was something missing: a moral code of behavior. Indeed, as we have seen, the gods often acted in a most immoral manner! Nor was there an earthly reward for virtue. The Greeks seem to have shrugged off every imaginable character weakness but one: excessive pride or arrogance (*hubris*). However, they did frown upon anyone who broke an oath or failed to honor the local gods. But given the lack of moral guidelines or spiritual appeal, many historians describe the Greek religion as little more than ceremonial bargaining with supernatural powers to obtain special favors.

There were few priests, since religious festivals and sacrifices were usually conducted by state officials. The principal duties of the priests were to look after the temples and to assist at services held there. At such private occasions as the birth of a child or a marriage, the head of the household led his family and friends in prayer.

A Greek temple was a simple rectangular stone structure with a pitched roof that was supported by pillars. Inside was a sanctuary containing a statue of a particular god or goddess. The building itself was considered the home of the deity rather than a place of worship. Religious ceremonies took place at an outside altar near the temple's entrance.

The Greek Concept of Death

When a Greek person died, the woman of the household washed the body and anointed it with olive oil, dressed it in white, and then placed a wreath upon its head. A funeral procession of mourners and flute players accompanied the body to its final resting place. A man was buried with such personal possessions as a spear, a shield, and farming tools. Women were often buried wearing their favorite pieces of jewelry and surrounded by cooking pots.

The Greeks believed that after death a person's soul went to the Underworld, the kingdom of Hades. To get there, it was first guided by Hermes to the banks of the River Styx. There a coin was given to Charon, the ferryman, to gain passage across the water (for this reason, a coin was always placed in the mouth of the dead body just before burial). On the other side of the Styx waited Cerberus, a three-headed dog whose duty was to stop the living from entering the Underworld and to prevent the dead from escaping. Once past Cerberus, the soul drank from the waters of another river, the Lethe; this caused it to forget about life on earth. When a person loses interest in life, he becomes tired and bored; the word "lethargy" is derived from Lethe. So is the word "lethal."

*fig. 43 — **Cerberus***

Next came a judgment of the quality of the deceased person's former life. The souls of wicked people were sent to Tartarus, a gloomy place where they were subjected to eternal discomfort. Most people ended up in the Asphodel Fields, a grey, boring region where they drifted about aimlessly in the shade, waiting for a living person to offer them a sacrifice (simply to break the monotony). This netherworld is vividly described by Homer in THE ODYSSEY. Truly virtuous people went to the Elysian Fields to live in golden sunlight forever. The soul of a virtuous person could be born again, and if it gained entry to the Elysian Fields three times it could advance to the Isles of the Blessed and share eternal happiness with Cronus and many other deities. Admission to this lofty realm was nearly impossible, but it provided a certain incentive to the Greeks to live respectable lives.

The Oracles

Throughout Greece there were many religious shrines called oracles where ordinary people could ask questions about the future; special priests at these shrines passed on the messages to the gods and then interpreted the divine responses.

There were over 250 oracles in Greece, but the most famous one was Apollo's temple at Delphi. This shrine was built on the slope of Mt. Parnassus, a rugged ridge rising 8,000 feet just north of the Gulf of Corinth. It was a most dramatic setting, and the Greeks considered it the center of the world.

There, in an underground chamber connected with the shrine, a priestess called the Pythia sat upon a golden stool. She breathed in vapors that rose up from a vent in the floor, frequently nibbling on laurel leaves at the same time. The vapors put her into a trance, during which she supposedly communicated directly with the god Apollo.

A visitor to Delphi was expected to sacrifice a goat outside the temple before entering the shrine. He then wrote down his question and gave it to the priests; they, in turn, posed the question to the Pythia. As she ranted and raved, they copied down her incoherent mutterings as best they could. Then they translated the "message from Apollo" into a rhymed prophecy and presented it to the visitor.

Military leaders and high-ranking government officials often came to the temple for advice before taking important actions, while common people asked more mundane questions, such as when to plant the next crop or whom to marry.

Predictions With Double Meanings

Sometimes it was difficult for the priests to know what was the best response. They realized that their oracle would lose its good reputation if they made too many inaccurate predictions, and so they gave answers that had double meanings. For example, when an Athenian general asked how to defend his city, the oracle advised seeking protection behind "wooden walls." But what were the wooden walls? Were they the walls of the city or the walls of a ship? We will discover which was the best answer in the next chapter.

Actually, the constant stream of visitors to Delphi taught the priests much of "world affairs," and they became very knowledgeable. As a result, their advice tended to be rather good.

Sometimes the oracle was extremely accurate. In 363 A.D. the Pythia announced that she would give no more predictions. And she was right! Soon afterwards the temple was ransacked by the Romans, and it gradually fell in ruins.

Other Oracles

Some Greek oracles used rather imaginative devices to predict the future, devices about as accurate as reading the tea leaves at the bottom of a cup! For example, at one oracle a man's fate depended upon whether a goat shook its head or simply stood quietly!

The oldest oracle was Dodona in Epirus, a stormy and mountainous region in northwestern Greece. This was a temple of Zeus, and the divine messages were issued from a sacred oak tree. The priests wrote the words on individual leaves, and these were carried by the wind to the person who had posed a question.

The Compatibility of Religion and Science

Their belief in the deities of Mt. Olympus did not prevent the Greeks from further exploring and questioning the order of the natural world. They saw no contradiction between religion and science, for they felt that by studying nature they were drawing closer to the divine powers that controlled everything. It was not until fairly late in the civilization of ancient Greece that significant numbers began to question the existence of the Olympians.

Questions:

1. According to the myths, who were the first Greek gods?
2. What prophecy worried Cronus?
3. How did Rhea protect Zeus?
4. How did Zeus and his two brothers divide up their father's kingdom?
5. In what ways were the gods and

goddesses less than perfect?

6. Who was Hesiod and why is he important?

7. Who was Cerberus?

8. What were the Elysian Fields?

9. How did the priests at the oracles solve the problem of finding acceptable answers to difficult questions?

10. How did the Greeks reconcile their religious beliefs with their respect for human reasoning?

Ideas to Think About

1. The Greeks created a society in which the individual had a say in how his life was governed. They had a positive attitude about the human potential, and so it is not surprising that their religion was based upon human-like deities. By thinking of their gods as being somewhat like themselves, only better, were they not also dreaming of the heights that they, as human beings, might attain?

2. Croesus, the king of Lydia in Asia Minor, once consulted the Oracle of Delphi to inquire whether he would win the war he was fighting. He was told that a great army would be destroyed. The king assumed that this meant that he would conquer his enemy. Unfortunately for him, it was his own army that was destroyed!

3. Many prophecies were delivered in bizarre ways. At an oracle in Thessaly, the visitor put a coin on the altar and burned incense. Then he put his fingers in his ears and ran off. At a certain distance from the shrine he removed his fingers from his ears. The first thing he heard anyone say about anything was supposed to be the answer to his question!

4. Tartarus was a horrible place of eternal punishment. The Tartars were a Mongolian tribe led by Genghis Khan in the twelfth century A.D. Their bloody and violent invasion of central Asia made that part of the earth seem as unpleasant a place as Tartarus was said to be. The similarity of these two words (Tartarus and tartar) that refer to something terrible is an interesting coincidence.

5. Deities that are believed to have a human shape are called *anthropomorphic* (a Greek word that means "assuming human form"). Belief in more than one god is called *polytheism* (a Greek word that means "many gods").

Projects:

1. There are many excellent books containing the Greek myths. Some are listed at the end of this book under SUGGESTED READINGS. Find one and read as many of the myths as you can. You will probably want to read them all!

2. Learn more about the creation of the world according to the religion of the early Greeks. Then draw a family tree, showing the relationships of the most important gods and goddesses.

3. According to an ancient myth, there was once a serpent called the Python that lived in a cave on Mt. Parnassus. It was slain by Apollo. The Pythia's name is derived from it. Find out more about the story and make a short report to the class.

4. Carved into the stone at the Oracle of Delphi are two famous expressions: "Know Thyself" and "Nothing In Excess." Choose one of the expressions and write a paragraph or two about what you think it means. Try to imagine yourself in ancient Greece as you consider the meaning.

5. Tantalus was the father of Pelops (remember Pelops' Island?). He was favored by the gods, and one night he invited some of them to dinner. He wanted to impress his immortal guests with a meal that was quite out of the ordinary. Find out what he served. Why were the gods so offended by his choice? How was he punished? What does the word "tantalize" mean?

6. This is a group project. Write a play based on one of the myths you have read. Feel free to modernize the expressions and the setting. Then present it to your class.

7. In ancient Greece *cosmos* meant order and harmony, the opposite of chaos. Today, cosmos refers to the universe (which the Greeks considered to be orderly), and cosmopolitan means "citizen of the world" (someone not restricted by local prejudices). Explain the meanings and derivations of these adjectives: gigantic, titanic, chaotic, and geometric. Use them in sentences. Can you think of any other words that come from Greek mythology?

Chapter X — THE PERSIAN WARS

A Common Enemy Unites Greece

Until the fifth century B.C., the city-states of mainland Greece remained aggressively independent. The only example of confederation on the entire peninsula was the Peloponnesian League headed by Sparta. It was not until all of Greece was threatened by a powerful foreign army that the city-states were forced to forget their petty squabbles and join together in defense of their homeland. This occurred when the armies of Persia invaded Greece.

We know a great deal about the period of the Persian Wars because the battles were described in great detail by the Greek historian Herodotus. He was the first person to attempt to write a thorough account of the important historical events of his time, and for this reason he is known as the Father of History. We shall refer to his writings from time to time.

A Mighty Empire

Persia was an ancient Asian civilization founded by nomads on the high plateaus of what is now Iran. In the mid-sixth century B.C. a Persian king named Cyrus began to extend his territory by conquering the lands of neighboring peoples. When he vanquished a tribe called the Medes, who had dominated western Asia up until then, he established the Persian Empire. It was Cyrus who defeated King Croesus of Lydia (see page 86 # 2). By 520 B.C. Cyrus's domain stretched from India westward to the bleak deserts of Libya, and from Egypt up to Thrace (the region just northeast of Greece). The distance from east to west was an incredible 2700 miles, and this made Persia the most extensive empire the world had ever seen. It was over one hundred times larger than Attica!

Persia In the Early Fifth Century

Darius I. came to power early in the fifth century B.C. Like all Persian monarchs, he was called "the Great King, King of kings ... king of this great earth far and wide." He divided his empire into twenty provinces called satrapies, each ruled by a governor (the satrap). Over the years, many of the satraps became very powerful men. Darius built a vast network of roads to

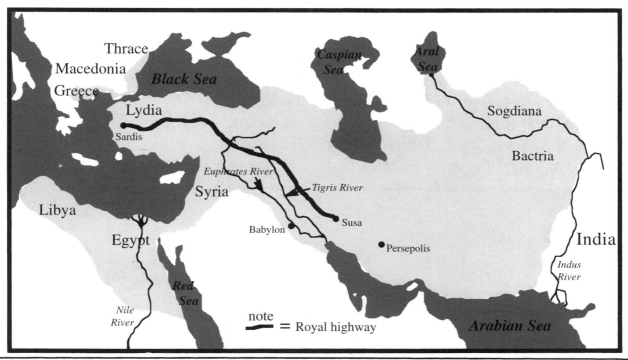

fig. 44 — The Persian Empire c. 490 BC

link the parts of his empire. The Royal Highway was a paved road that ran 1500 miles from Susa (near the Persian Gulf) to Sardis (near the Aegean Sea).

The peoples who had been conquered by the Persians were forced to pay Darius tribute (a kind of tax) and to serve in the Persian army (the Persian people themselves paid no taxes at all). This subjugation was particularly unbearable for the freedom-loving Greeks whose cities in Ionia had been conquered by the armies of Cyrus a half century earlier.

The Ionian Revolt

In 499 B.C. Aristagoras of Miletus led the Ionians in a revolt against Darius. The Greeks refused to pay any more tribute or to serve in the Persian army. They appealed to their countrymen in mainland Greece to help them. Athens and Eretria (a city-state near Athens on the island of Euboea) responded with aid; Athens sent twenty ships and Eretria contributed five.

Together the Ionian and mainland Greeks attacked Sardis, the base of the local Persian satrap. After sacking the city, the mainland Greeks departed—no one is certain why. They probably thought that they had no chance against the Persian army. Left to defend themselves as best they could, the rebels were easily defeated; their small fleet of ships was destroyed and the city of Miletus was set afire. The Persians showed no mercy toward the city that had started the rebellion; many of the Greek boys were mutilated, the prettiest girls were sent as gifts to Darius, and the surviving soldiers were sentenced to exile in the far-off regions of central Persia.

Darius was furious that the mainland Greeks had supported the Ionians, and he was determined to punish them

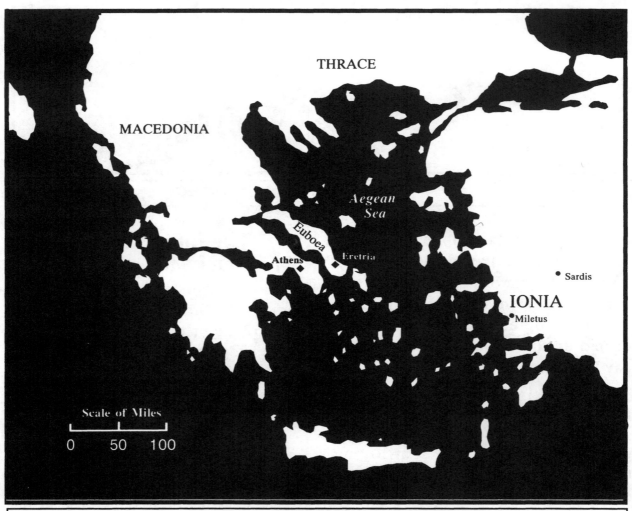

*fig. 45 — **Ancient Greece and Ionia***

for meddling in his affairs. He promptly dispatched an army and a fleet to subdue mainland Greece; the army was under the command on his son-in-law, Mardonius. To their surprise, the Persians encountered violent resistance from the tribes of warriors living in Thrace and Macedonia (north of Greece). Mardonius was wounded, and to make matters worse, the Persian fleet was partially destroyed in a sudden storm. Darius' army had no choice but to return home.

Darius Tests the Waters

In the spring of 492 B.C. Darius sent envoys to Greece to assess the degree of Greek opposition to Persian authority. His men solicited offerings of earth and water (this traditional gesture symbolized acceptance of a foreign government on land and sea), and the requests were granted by many city-states. Athens and Sparta felt differently, however. Herodotus tells us that the unfortunate envoy sent to Athens was unceremoniously thrown into a ditch and told to gather his own dirt! Similarly, the Spartans responded to Darius' demand by heaving the Persian into a well, telling him to swallow as much water as he wished!

Invasion

In 490 B.C. Darius summoned an army of some of his best warriors and sailed with them directly across the Aegean Sea to Greece. The Persians seized several Greek islands on the way.

Darius' first goal was to destroy the port city of Eretria, whose soldiers had participated in the burning of Sardis. From there he would march about thirty miles south to deal with Athens. When his soldiers landed on the island of Euboea, the local citizens staged a heroic resistance, but they were hopelessly outnumbered. Eretria was sacked and burned. A narrow strait separated Euboea from the mainland.

The Plain of Marathon

*fig. 46 — **The area of Marathon***

As smoke filled the eastern sky, the Persians sailed across the calm waters and landed on the plain of Marathon.

A Summons for Help

The Athenian army raced northward to meet the invaders. The Greek soldiers must have trembled at the sight of the tall, fierce-looking Asian warriors who outnumbered them two to one! Miltiades, the Athenian general, had previously encountered Persian might while fighting in Thrace, and it was clear to him that the Athenians needed the help of the Spartan soldiers, the best fighters in all of Greece. A messenger named Pheidippides was immediately recruited to run to Sparta for aid; he covered the distance of 150 miles in only two days. But the timing couldn't have been worse! The Spartans were involved in a religious festival (in honor of Apollo), and they would send no soldiers to Marathon until their ceremonies ended at the next full moon. Pheidippides then raced back to Marathon with the discouraging news.

A second runner was sent to Plataea, a city-state in Boeotia, with a similar request for aid. That city responded with a force of six hundred men.

The Advantage of a Well-Armed Hoplite

Despite their fewer numbers, the Greeks did have some advantages as they faced the Persians. First of all, their footsoldiers were extremely well armed. Each man carried a six-foot spear (used for thrusting, not throwing) as well as a short sword. Furthermore, he was protected by bronze armor: a helmet adorned with a crest of dyed horsehair, a molded breast-plate and greaves (which covered his lower leg). He carried a heavy round wooden shield called a *hoplon*; this explains why Greek footsoldiers were called *hoplites*. The hoplon was about three feet wide, bulging slightly outward toward the center but flat around the rim, where it was reinforced with a strip of bronze. A metal armband attached to the inner side helped the hoplite to hold the shield steady.

The Persians were considerably less

fig. 47 — **A hoplite**

well protected. They carried large wicker (wooden) shields covered with leather, and these could be easily pierced. They had no helmets (they simply wore cloth headdresses), nor did they wear body armor. Furthermore. they carried spears that were far shorter than those of the Greek hoplites. The one advantage the Persians had, apart from their superior numbers, was the much-renowned skill of their archers.

The Greek Phalanx

The greatest asset of the Greek army was its unique battle formation. Fighting strategies had changed drastically since the days of the Trojan War, when warrior heroes had ridden to battle in chariots and then dismounted to engage in hand-to-hand combat. Now the Greek hoplites marched shoulder to shoulder in a tight-knit configuration called a *phalanx*, one row of men directly behind another. The soldiers were protected by the solid line of their shields.

As the phalanx marched forward, the spears of the front rank were extended forward like the quills of a giant porcupine. Although the spear of a single soldier could be easily dealt with by an opponent, a long unbroken line of thrust spears was an intimidating sight.

The Greek soldiers moved as a single unit, responding without hesitation to the orders of their commander. On the battlefield a phalanx would march steadily forward to the sound of a flute until it made physical contact with the opposing line of soldiers. As the men in the front ranks thrust their spears, they were pushed forward by the weight of the rest of the hoplites marching behind them. Thus a battle was basically a shoving match, and the winner was the side that broke through the opposing line. Those men in the front ranks who fell were immediately replaced by those marching behind them. The phalanx was not a rigid formation; it could adopt different configurations, varying from a long thin line strung out across a wide field to a deep concentration only a few soldiers wide traversing a narrow mountain pass.

Since the soldiers carried their shields in their left hands, the right side of a phalanx was vulnerable, and one popular strategy was to attack an enemy phalanx on that side. Sometimes wealthy Greek soldiers mounted on horses formed a cavalry that protected the vulnerable flanks of the phalanx and later chased retreating enemy soldiers.

The Greek phalanx required con-

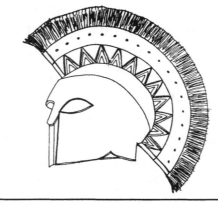

fig. 48 — **A hoplite's helmet**

stant training and strict discipline. It represented a team effort, and it was an incredibly effective offensive formation against any army that fought in the traditional free-for-all style of soldier against soldier.

A final Greek advantage was a psychological one: The hoplites were fighting to defend their homeland against an invading enemy, and the

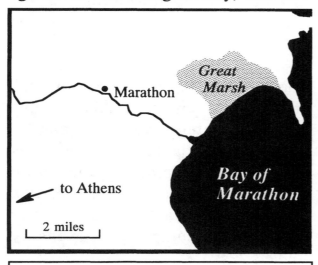

fig. 49 — **Site of Marathon**

sense of patriotism that filled their ranks fueled their determination to use every ounce of energy and strength against the foreign troops.

The Battle Begins

Miltiades commanded an army of ten thousand Athenians and six hundred Plateans against Persia's force of twenty thousand. (Herodotus's descriptions of one hundred thousand Persians was greatly exaggerated!) Despite the overwhelming odds, he knew he had no choice but to attack (he could hardly wait for the Spartans). He tried to compensate for his small numbers by thinly stretching his front line across the width of the plain and reducing the depth of the phalanx from eight ranks of men to four.

At the signal from their general, the Greek soldiers shouted their war cry to muster their courage and then charged. They crossed the plain at a run, thus making difficult targets for the enemy archers who were accustomed to slower moving opponents. The Persians must have been startled by the forceful assault, but nonetheless they fought hard and aggressively.

The Persian center stood its ground. However, Miltiades had placed his best troops on the two flanks, and these soldiers fought with such courage and force that they routed the opposing enemy wings. The Greek flanks then wheeled around to attack the enemy center from behind. The stunned Persian soldiers found themselves surrounded by gleaming Greek spears and swords! The Athenians fought on with a ferocity that would have impressed even the Spartans. In a short time, they were masters of the field. Many of the retreating Persian soldiers got bogged down in a salt marsh that lay between the field of battle and the beach; a large number of them drowned, while others raced frantically toward their waiting ships.

No one could have predicted the Greek victory at Marathon, and Miltiades must have been ecstatic! In a triumph of cunning and teamwork over brute strength, he had lost only 192 men to the Persians' 6,400! When the Spartans later arrived at the battlefield, they gazed silently upon the scene of the Athenian victory. They were justifiably impressed.

The Greek dead were later buried in a common grave; the mound can still be seen today. Veterans of the battle were highly honored in their city-states for the rest of their lives.

The First Marathon Race

According to legend, Miltiades sent a runner, the same Pheidippides who had raced to Sparta, to carry news of the victory to Athens. The message would also warn the city to close its gates to any Persian forces in the region. Exhausted by all the running he had done as well as the day's battle, the gallant messenger had only enough strength left as he staggered through the city's gate to gasp, "Rejoice, victory is ours!" Then he fell down—dead. The twenty odd miles he had run from Marathon to Athens has become the model for modern footraces, called marathons, over a similar distance. (In a less romantic version of this story, a runner other than Pheidippides carried the message to Athens.)

fig. 50 — **Pheidippides**

1212 427 34 32

The Persians Withdraw

Meanwhile, the Greek army proceeded to the outskirts of Athens to take up defensive positions. The Persian fleet was undoubtedly unsettled by the array of soldiers lining the shore; the enemy ships hastily picked up their straggling troops and withdrew to Asia.

The Athenians were overjoyed! They had proven that their determined hoplites could stand up against as mighty a foe as the Persian army. But they worried that they had not seen the last of their enemy. As it turned out, they had simply won breathing time.

The Greeks Strengthen Their Defenses

The Persian invasion made it clear to the Greeks that they had to take precautions against future attacks. In the interest of self-preservation, thirty-one city-states formed an alliance, promising to aid each other if they were threatened by outside forces. This new Panhellenic ("all Greek") League included the members of the Peloponnesian League.

After the death of Miltiades, the Athenian forces were placed under the command of a wise politician named Themistocles. He believed that the city needed a strong navy to defend itself.

The timely discovery of veins of silver in the hills of Attica helped Athens to finance the building of a fleet of two hundred ships.

A Giant Army

Darius died soon after his crushing defeat at Marathon, but his son Xerxes never forgot his father's humiliating loss, and he vowed to avenge it. In 480 B.C., ten years after Marathon, Xerxes invaded Europe with a huge army of 180,000 soldiers. Herodotus estimated the figure at over two million, but scholars agree that, once again, the historian exaggerated. Nonetheless, this was the largest armed force ever assembled. The troops came from many parts of the Persian empire—there were Babylonians, Armenians, Lydians, Syrians, Egyptians, Libyans, and many tribesmen. The soldiers seemed a motley crew with their differing styles of dress and types of weapons, and they spoke a wide variety of languages.

A Bridge Connects Asia to Europe

Xerxes moved his vast army across the 3/4 mile wide expanse of waters of the Hellespont by lashing together over six hundred boats to build a double pontoon bridge. Two rows of boats were lined up side-by-side; they were held in place by great boulders of rock that had been tied to long ropes and thrown into the sea bed (they were primitive but effective anchors). Other ropes joined the ships together. Wooden planks were then placed across the hulls of the ships and layed across the ropes that held the vessels together. The result was a long wooden bridge stretching across the ships from shore to shore. The planks were covered with dirt and straw to fill in the gaps between them, and canvas sails were layered over the side railings. These measures prevented the horses and cattle that were led across the bridge from seeing the sea and stampeding. They must have allayed the fears of the soldiers as well! It took seven days and seven nights for Xerxes' entire army to march across the double bridge.

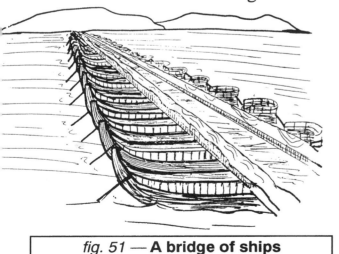

fig. 51 — A bridge of ships

The Move Toward Greece

When they were safely ashore on European soil, the Persian army began making its way across Thrace toward Thessaly. The soldiers were supplied by the fleet of ships that followed them along the coast, although rumors circulated in Greece that the enemy troops were drinking the rivers dry!

To avoid the dangerous waters at the cape of Mount Athos (Mardonius had lost many ships there ten years earlier), Xerxes ordered that a canal be dug across the isthmus, a distance of a mile and a quarter. Traces of the canal are still visible today.

An Ambiguous Prediction

Meanwhile, Athenians were busily preparing for the worst. They consulted the Oracle of Delphi, asking the Pythia how they could best defend their city against the Persians. To their horror, the oracle predicted disaster and advised the Athenians to flee for their lives! The only hope, it added, lay in "the wooden walls" (see page 85). As usual, the oracle's message was vague and offered multiple interpretations. What were the wooden walls? Some men thought of the wooden palisade that surrounded the Acropolis, and they concluded that the city's population should seek shelter behind them.

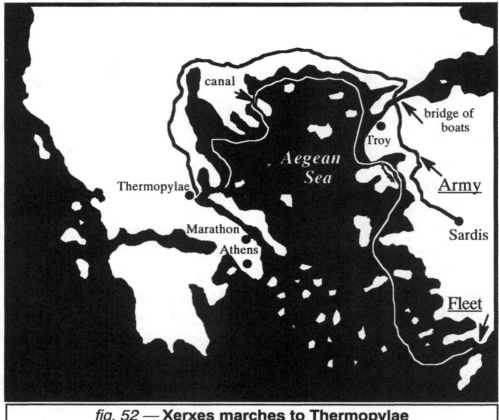

fig. 52 — **Xerxes marches to Thermopylae**

Themistocles, however, was convinced that the wooden walls were the sides of his newly built fleet of ships. He believed that the Athenians' only hope for survival against the Persians lay with their navy.

The Greek Strategy

As the enemy troops moved closer to Greece, the Athenians and the Spartans formed a coalition: Athens agreed to send her fleet against the enemy warships, while the Spartans were to take command on the fields of battle. Everyone agreed that this was an excellent division of resources.

The Greeks decided to make a stand against the Persians at the Pass of Thermopylae ("the gate by the hot springs") on the southern border of Thessaly. This narrow piece of beach between a sheer mountain wall and the sea was the major route from north to south. The Spartans knew that their numbers were greatly inferior to those of the vast Persian army, and they hoped to lessen their disadvantage by bunching their men as tightly as

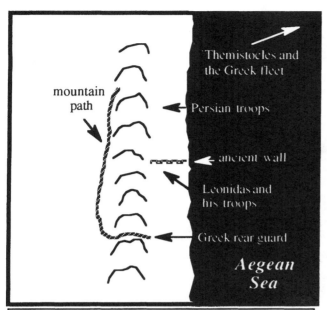

fig. 53 — Thermopylae as the battle begins

possible in the 50-foot-wide pass. Since only a limited number of enemy soldiers could crowd onto the beach at one time, the Greek hoplites had a reasonable chance of holding their line against the invaders.

The Greek army that assembled at Thermopylae was led by Leonidas, king of Sparta. His eight thousand soldiers included three hundred members of the Spartan royal body-guard. He posted one thousand men at the southern entry to the pass to protect the rear of his army. When one of the Spartans heard a Persian envoy warn that the arrows of the enemy archers would darken the sky, he confidently replied, "So much the better. We can fight in the shade!"

Themistocles commanded the fleet that was moored just north of the island of Euboea near Artemisium. The plan was for the Athenian ships to engage in frequent skirmishes on the high seas in an effort to prevent the Persian vessels from supplying their troops with food and weapons.

Xerxes' army waited near the pass for four days. Perhaps the generals were sizing up the Greek forces and planning their strategies. On the fifth day the Persians attacked. Leonidas and his men were ready. Manning an ancient wall, they ably repulsed every attempted assault. When the same thing happened the next day, Xerxes must have wondered how he could turn things around to his own advantage. It was at this opportune moment that a Greek traitor named Ephialtes informed Xerxes of a mountain path leading to the other side of the pass behind the Spartans—just where Leonidas had placed his rear guard! That night, the heartless scoundrel (undoubtedly he was promised a large reward) person-ally led a contingent of Persians over the mountain; a full moon made it easy for them to follow the path. The sleeping Greek guard was caught by surprise and easily routed.

A Valiant Stand

When Leonidas learned of the defeat of his rear guard, he hastily sent away most of his soldiers. He realized that he was trapped and that his cause was hopeless, but at least he could give his retreating men a chance to reach the safety of their comrades further south. According to legend, he told his remaining warriors to have a good breakfast, for later "we shall dine in (the kingdom of) Hades!"

Heroically, he led his own Spartan troops against what must have seemed like an infinite number of Persian soldiers. Herodotus describes how valiantly the Greeks fought, using their fists when their weapons were gone. In the end, their dead bodies were heaped upon each other at the entrance to the pass. Only two survived—one would be killed at a subsequent battle against the Persians, and the other killed himself on the spot at Thermopylae. For him the humiliation of defeat was too great to bear. Yet, the Spartans had held off the enemy long enough to insure the safe withdrawal of the rest of the Greek soldiers.

Although the Persians won the pass at Thermopylae, the reports of the courage of Leonidas and his men inspired the rest of the Greek army to pick up their fallen standard. To this day Leonidas is remembered as one of history's most gallant military leaders. A bronze statue of the Spartan king now guards the narrow pass. Nearby, a stone marker bears this moving epitaph to him and his three hundred warriors: "Go, stranger, and tell them in Sparta that we lie here in obedience to their orders."

The Destruction of Athens

When Themistocles heard of the massacre at Thermopylae, he immediately took the fleet south. The Persians, buoyed by their victory, marched triumphantly through the pass and then set up headquarters near Thebes. When they stormed the city of Athens, they found it nearly deserted. Most Athenians had fled and sought refuge on the island of Salamis and in Troezen (a city in the eastern Peloponnese). The Persian soldiers were greeted by the howling of abandoned dogs. Some of the pets did manage to escape, however. One account describes how a dog belonging to the family of the statesman Pericles (we'll learn more about him later) followed the retreating Athenians and even swam across the strait of Salamis, only to collapse and die from exhaustion on the island beach.

The Persians savagely killed the

handful of men who had chosen to remain to defend their city, burned the temples on the Acropolis and greedily plundered the shops and houses. They even burned Athena's sacred olive tree. (When the tree later sent out new green shoots, it became a symbol of the resilience of the Greek people.) The Athenians who had fled watched helplessly as the smoke from their burning city filled the evening sky.

The Battle of Salamis

The strait of water separating Salamis from the mainland of Greece is narrow and treacherous. As the Greek fleet waited nearby for the inevitable attack by the Persians, the wily Themistocles thought of a scheme to gain the upper hand. He sent a soldier to Xerxes under the guise of a traitor; the man was to tell the Persian king that the Greek sailors were terrified of the enemy forces and were on the verge of retreat. Xerxes snatched the bait, and he immediately ordered his ships to sail to Salamis and attack the Greeks. He expected an easy victory.

The Greek Advantage

The Greek ships were called triremes because they had three (*tri* means three in Greek) banks of fourteen-foot oars. One hundred and seventy rowers stroked the huge oars and kept in time by listening to the rhythmical sounds of a flute. A metal-ended battering ram extended below the waterline in the prow of each ship. In battle, a ship was rowed at top speed toward the side of an enemy vessel; as the battering ram crashed through the hull, it created a huge hole that caused the hold to fill with water. The hapless rowers of a sinking ship were then speared by the soldiers on the deck of the attacking vessel. Effective ramming depended upon the captain's mastery of force and speed; if the ship went too fast the ram would wedge too deeply and become stuck, while a slow approach would enable the enemy to get away. After ramming, a ship had to back up quickly so that the enemy sailors couldn't board its decks. An alternative strategy was to race parallel to an enemy vessel; just before pulling along side, the captain would order his oarsmen to pull in their oars. The attacking ship would then

fig. 54 — **A trireme**

crash through the oars of the enemy vessel, breaking them as though they were matchsticks!

Like Leonidas, Themistocles seized the advantage in spite of the smaller numbers of his forces by fighting in a confined area. The Greek sailors knew the channels and hidden reefs of their own waters better than an invading enemy possibly could, and their ships were nimbler. They couldn't expect to win a battle against the huge Persian fleet on the open seas, but the narrow strait of Salamis was a different matter.

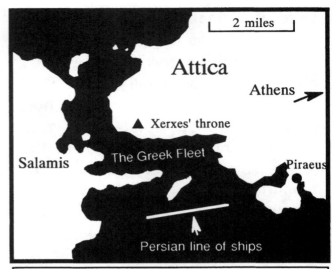

fig. 55 — **The Battle of Salamis**

The Attack

When the Persian ships arrived at the strait, they quickly formed a solid line and moved slowly and deliberately toward the narrow row of Greek triremes guarding the entrance. The Greeks ships were outnumbered three to one. Xerxes, fully confident of a victory, had his golden throne set upon a hillside overlooking the strait. From there he planned to enjoy observing the destruction of the Greek navy.

Slowly, Themistocles' ships began to back water, the rowers softly chanting a hymn to Apollo. The Persians were delighted to see the Greeks withdrawing into the strait. They assumed that, as the "traitor" had predicted, the pathetic Greek captains were

faltering in courage and attempting a slow and cowardly retreat. Responding to the shouts of their leaders, the Persian oarsmen rowed energetically, rapidly advancing toward the center of the continuously retreating Greek line. Soon the entire Persian fleet had been lured into the narrow strait. Themistocles now had the upper hand!

As the blare of a trumpet cut through the air, the Greeks attacked, crashing into the enemy vessels closest to the shores and driving the bewildered Persians into the center of the strait. Total confusion raged among Xerxes' captains as their ships smashed against each other. The Athenian seamen, anxious to avenge their still smoldering city, furiously rammed their triremes against the sides of the trapped vessels, breaking their oars, flooding their galleys, and driving them onto the rocks that lined the channel. Ship-wrecked Persian seamen were stabbed like fish by the triumphant Greeks!

A Hasty Departure

Xerxes watched in horror as half of his ships were destroyed. Those Persian vessels that survived the onslaught quickly withdrew, signaling a total victory for the Greeks. The "Great King" led the bulk of his army back to the Hellespont and across the bridges to Asia. Persian messengers sailed across the Aegean and sped along the Royal Road from Sardis to Susa, bearing the news of the fiasco. Herodotus described how "neither snow, nor rain, nor heat, nor gloom of night stayed these couriers from the swift completion of their appointed rounds." If these words sound familiar, it is because they have become the unofficial motto of the U.S. Post Office!

Xerxes left behind a part of his army (about 70,000 men) under the command of his brother-in-law Mardo-nius. They were ordered to winter in Thessaly and to resume the attack the following year. (In those days, wars only took place during the good weather!) Meanwhile, the Greeks reveled in their victory.

The End of the War

The following summer (479 B.C.), a Spartan king named Pausanias led an army against the Persian troops at the plain of Plataea on Boeotia's southern border (Pausanias was the regent for Leonida' son). As usual, the Greeks were outnumbered, but the Spartans led them to victory. Mardonius was killed, as were most of his footsoldiers. Pausanias thus avenged Leonidas' defeat at Thermopylae, and once and for all the hated Persians were driven out of Greece. Herodotus noted with uncharacteristic understatement that the Persians "departed with altered minds" about the abilities of the Greek army and navy!

The same day as the battle of Platea, Greek triremes attacked and burned the Persian fleet while it was beached at Mycale on the coast of Anatolia. Afterwards, they moved on to free the Aegean islands and the Ionian cities from Persian rule.

The Persian Wars had come to an end, and the Spartan army and Athenian fleet were acknowledged as invincible forces throughout the Mediterranean world. In a surging spirit of patriotism, all the Greeks rejoiced at what they had accomplished. Had they not driven the world's mightiest army from their native soil? Throughout

Greece every citizen was filled with pride and confidence, and the future looked bright indeed.

Questions:

1. Who was Herodotus?
2. Why did the Ionian city-states revolt?
3. Why did Darius invade Greece?
4. What advantages did the Greek soldiers have over the Persians?
5. Describe the first marathon.
6. What was the prediction of the Oracle of Delphi regarding the Persian invasion?
7. Why did the Greeks lose at Thermopylae?
8. Describe a trireme.
9. How did Themistocles lure the Persian ships into the narrow strait?
10. Who finally drove the Persians out of Greece?

Ideas To Think About

1. The distance between Marathon and Athens is a little over twenty miles. When a "marathon race" was run in London in the last century, the distance was increased to twenty-six miles so that the course would go by Winsor Palace! It has remained a race of twenty-six miles ever since.

2. When the Persians first arrived at Thermopylae, Xerxes sent a spy around the mountains to observe the Greek camp. He came back with the report that the Spartans were doing exercises and combing their long hair. At first the Persian king laughed at the image of such seemingly effeminate behavior, but his mood changed when one of his men informed him that the Spartans were the most valiant warriors in the land and that they always ceremoniously combed their long hair before fighting to the death.

3. From the start, the Greeks had little respect for the Persian culture. The Athenians in particular considered the Persian people little more than slaves ordered about by a tyrannical ruler. Didn't the Persian subjects approach their king on their knees? The Greeks didn't even kneel for their gods! The evolving Greek ideas about self-government and the worth of each individual contrasted dramatically with the Persians' unquestioning submission to their king. While the Greeks were bound together by a common language, religion and set of customs, apparently the Persian empire could only be kept in line by the iron hand of a powerful monarch. When Darius invaded Greece, the defense of a new concept of

government was at stake. If the Persians had won the war, the Greek experiment in democracy would very likely have been snuffed out.

4. The average Greek hoplite carried nearly seventy pounds of equipment into battle. Remember that he had a heavy wooden shield and a long spear in addition to his armor and smaller weapons. It was thus crucial for him to spend a part of each day doing exercises that would build up his stamina. No wonder a strong body was considered one of the hallmarks of the ideal Greek man.

5. Actually, Xerxes' engineers had to construct two different sets of pontoon bridges. The first set was smashed by a violent storm that blew across the Mediterranean. Xerxes was furious, and he ordered the Hellespont punished! The waves were given three hundred lashes with a whip, branded with hot irons, and fettered (a pair of shackles was thrown into the water). And the engineers who built the bridges were beheaded!

6. The Immortals were an elite corps of the Persian army. Ten thousand of the best soldiers were hand-picked to serve in the corps. When one man was

injured or killed, he was immediately replaced. This explains how they got their name. Xerxes' special bodyguard numbered one thousand Immortals; each had a golden apple attached to the end of his spear. The other nine thousand had silver apples on their spears.

*fig. 56 — **An early Greek helmet***

Projects:

1. On a large piece of poster board draw a trireme. This can be an outer view or a cross-section. Consult books in the classroom or library for a good picture to copy. Label all the important parts of the ship.

2. Learn more about the Persian army. Make a chart, comparing and contrasting the weapons and fighting techniques of the Greeks and the Persians.

3. The first great historical account of a war was Herodotus' description of the

Persian Wars. He was extremely interested in the causes of the east-west (Europe vs. Asia) conflict. Titled THE HISTORY, a copy of this work is available in most large libraries. Find a copy and select some passages to read to the class.

4. Cyrus I. was one of Persia's greatest monarchs. Find out about him and write a short report.

5. Not long after his victory, Themistocles was ostracized from his city. Where did he end up living until his death? Write a paragraph about his final days.

6. Croesus, King of Lydia, conquered Ionia, only to be conquered by Cyrus I. of Persia. We have already read about his predicaments (see page 86). Find out more about this fascinating man, and write a short report.

7. At the conclusion of the Persian Wars, Athens and Sparta were the two "superpowers" of Greece. Yet, the governments and basic attitudes of the two city-states could not have been more opposite. Before reading any further, write a short essay describing what you think will probably happen next, once the Athenian and Spartan fighters have returned to their native soil. Be imaginative, and back up your statements with solid reasons.

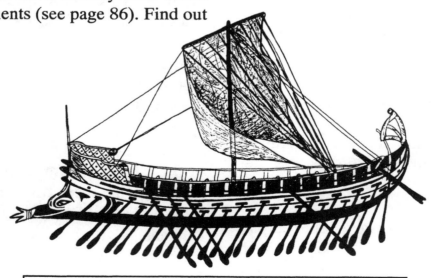

*fig. 57 — **An early model of a trireme***

Chapter XI — THE OLYMPIC GAMES

Early Religious Festivals

The Greeks held many festivals to honor their gods and goddesses. In fact, there were over seventy festival days each year. The most famous celebration was held in honor of Zeus every four years in Olympia, a religious sanctuary dedicated to the king of gods in the northwestern Peloponnese. Olympia lay nestled in a valley at the junction of two rivers near the foot of a hill named for Cronus.

The festival at Olympia was not only religious in nature. It was also a time for socializing and merry-making, and the acrobats, food peddlers, and athletic competitions created the atmosphere of a modern country fair. As more attention was focused upon the sporting events, the festival came to be known as the Olympic Games. Actually, competitive sports had long been a tradition even in those early times; they are vividly described in both of Homer's epics.

The Olympic Games were first held in July, 776 B.C., and they took place regularly for over one thousand years. The four-year period between festivals was known as an Olympiad; the Olympiads were numbered consecutively, and this division of time served as a useful system for dating important historical events in Greece.

fig. 58 — **Carian Zeus**
H.L. Pierce Fund — Courtesy, Museum of Fine Arts, Boston

The Evolution of the Olympic Games

At first only one athletic event was held at Zeus's festival: This was a 186 yard sprint (called the *dromos*) in which swift young men demonstrated their physical ability by dashing across a field and back again. The purpose of the race was to pay homage to Zeus. The first winner was a cook named Coroibos from the nearby town of Elis.

For fifty years the dromos remained the only athletic event at the festival, but eventually other races were added. When the Spartans took an active interest in the competitions, the program was further expanded to include a wide variety of contests. Actually, "athlete" comes from the Greek word *athlos* which means "contest." Over the years, the Olympic Games evolved into a long series of athletic competitions that were interspaced with religious ceremonies and literary presentations. By the fifth century, the festival had expanded to five days.

A National Celebration

The Olympic Games eventually became so popular that during the week in mid-summer when they were held all fighting between city-states throughout Greece came to a halt. A national truce allowed the athletes to travel safely to Olympia, participate in the events, and then return to their stations on the battlefield! This was known as the Sacred Truce.

Contestants had to be of Greek lineage, and they came from as far away as Sicily and Ionia. Women were not allowed to attend the games (the athletes competed in the nude!), but male slaves were welcome to observe the events. Greek women later created their own games called the *Heraea* (in honor of Hera) which were held every five years. These included running events for girls of different ages.

The Stadium

The Olympic running races took place on a wide track known as the stadium. The term "stadium" comes from the Greek word *stade*, meaning "one length of the track." Over 20,000 spectators could watch the races from the grassy embankments surrounding the stadium.

The long stretch of track had starting and finish lines at the two ends. The runners fitted their toes into grooved marble slabs. These were history's first starting blocks, and they can still be seen today in the ruins of the stadium. A blast of a trumpet signaled the beginning of a race. The clay surface was covered with sand to give the runners traction. According to Greek legend, the track measured six hundred feet because this was the distance that the legendary super-hero Heracles could run with one lungful of air.

The Other Events

Among the most popular Olympic events were the throwing of the discus (a nine to twelve-pound circular plate of bronze resembling a modern frisbee), the hurling of the javelin (a long spear), wrestling matches (no holds barred!), and boxing (without padded gloves). There was also a standing broad jump in which the athlete grasped metal weights in his hands for added momentum.

Greek hoplites had to be in top physical condition to fight in a phalanx, and the ideal of the athletic soldier was dramatically demonstrated in a twelve hundred-foot dash in which the runners wore helmets and carried heavy shields. They must have felt incredibly encumbered!

fig. 59 — **A discus thrower**

The Pancratium

A very odd and violent event was called the pancratium; it was a wild, free-for-all fight in which a contestant could box, wrestle, spit, kick and do just about anything except bite or gouge out his opponent's eyes! The word pancratium means "all powers," and the athletes were probably huge and burly strongmen resembling our modern wrestlers. Milo of Crotono became a national hero because he won the pancratium seven times; he claimed that he developed his great strength by carrying a calf for an hour every day until it was a full grown bull!

The fight continued until one man held up his hand in defeat. Occasionally, there was a fight to the death. Arrachion of Phigalia, the winner of two previous pancratium crowns, died in a stranglehold; however, his dead body was awarded the victor's crown!

Not all wrestling events were this dangerous. In upright wrestling, a competitor simply had to throw his opponent to the ground three times; in ground wrestling, the two men struggled until one of them was pinned. The wrestling events took place in an arena called the *palaistra*.

Horse Racing

Chariot racing was later added to the games, and the crowd was encouraged to wage bets on their favorites. The horses raced on a special oval track called a *hippodrome*. A wooden post marked the turning point at each end of the track. The chariots were pulled by teams of either two or four horses (depending upon the event), and a race consisted of twelve laps around the two posts. To begin the race, the horses lined up in a starting gate. These races were extremely dangerous; collisions and upsets were frequent occurrences. In one race, out of forty starters only one chariot finished!

In other races at the hippodrome the horses were ridden bareback by jockeys. One unusual event required the jockey to dismount at a certain point and run the last stretch while leading his horse! Many of the best horses came from Macedonia, a kingdom to the north of Greece. Although the Greeks considered the Macedonians crude and uncivilized, they allowed them to attend the Olympic Games so that they could view their magnificent steeds. In 356 B.C. King Philip II. of Macedonia entered a stallion in a race at Olympia and won. On the same day his son Alexander was born. Philip thought that his victory was a good omen for his son, as indeed it was. We shall learn more of Alexander later.

The Pentathlon

The Greeks believed that it was important to excel in many areas, to be "well-rounded" rather than to specialize in only one skill. This ideal was reflected in the *pentathlon*, a grueling competition of five events. The word pentathlon means "five contests," and these included a footrace (a two hundred-yard dash), a discus throw, a long jump, a javelin throw, and wrestling. Contestants were eliminated in each event, and the victor of the last contest was the overall winner—the "pentathlete." This was the highest honor attainable at the Olympic Games.

The Cultural Events

Between the athletic competitions poets read their works and orators recited speeches about every subject imaginable. On one occasion, the historian Herodotus read numerous pages of his famous accounts of the Persian Wars to an attentive audience! There were also contests between trumpeters, heralds, and painters.

An Emphasis On Sportsmanship

The rules of the games were very precise, and it was considered a matter of personal honor to strictly adhere to them. Before any events took place, the athletes (and their trainers) swore an oath at the altar of Zeus to abide by the regulations and to practice good sportsmanship. The judges, resplendent in their purple robes, swore that they would accept no bribes!

Anyone found guilty of breaking a rule was eliminated from competition and forced to pay a fine. This was, of course, a great humiliation. The fine money was used to erect copper statues of Zeus (called *Zanes*), the bases of which were engraved with the names of athletes found guilty of cheating. The statues lined the entrance to the stadium and served as a reminder to the contestants to remain honest!

The Awards

Upon conclusion of the athletic competitions, a procession of the champions as well as the judges marched to the Temple of Zeus. There the victorious athletes received garlands of wild olive branches cut with a golden knife from the trees of the sacred olive grove that grew near the temple. Even the statue of Zeus was crowned with a wreath of olive branches to signify his victory over the Titans.

After the awards ceremonies, the winners and other contestants feasted on the meat of hundreds of animals that had been sacrificed to Zeus, washing down the delicious food with liberal amounts of wine.

fig. 60 — **A winner's wreath**

All Hail the Conquering Hero!

Olympic champions were considered heroes in their native city-states. Upon his return home, a victor traditionally drove a chariot pulled by four white horses through a special opening made in the city wall. He then placed his olive wreath on the altar of the patron god of his city. Afterwards, a banquet was held in his honor. Many champions enjoyed free meals for life! A Spartan victor won the right to stand by his king in battle; for a warrior, this was the ultimate honor.

Sculptors made statues of the winning athletes, and these were proudly displayed throughout their home cities. Poets (the most famous was Pindar of Thebes) wrote odes in tribute to the champions.

Other Games

Although the games at Olympia were the most prestigious athletic contests, the Greeks held many other important festivals that included sporting events. Those competitions that were open to all Greeks were known as panhellenic ("all-Greek") games.

The Pythian Games were held in honor of Apollo every four years in the middle of each Olympiad at Delphi. Winners received crowns of laurel leaves, since the laurel was sacred to Apollo. The Pythian Games were especially famous for their competitions of lyre and flute players as well as their contests for original musical compositions (remember, Apollo was the god of music). These more creative events alternated with the usual running, jumping, and throwing competitions.

Every two years athletic games were held at Nemea and Corinth. The Nemean victors wore wreaths of wild parsley or celery, while those at the Isthmian Games in Corinth (held in honor of Poseidon) won wreaths of pine needles.

Athens was the site of the Panathenaic games. Most participants in these events were from Attica, but other Greeks were welcome as well. A winner was given an amphora (clay jar) filled with olive oil; this was an appropriate award, since, as we have learned, clay pottery and olive oil were the chief products of Athens. The amphora was decorated with a painting of the particular event in which it was won. This is the source of our modern tradition of awarding large cups to the winners of sporting tournaments.

Smaller local festivals offered a variety of other awards, including pottery jars filled with wine, armor, weapons, and even money.

The End of the Olympic Games

The Olympic Games were held every four years until 394 A.D. By that time Greece had been conquered by the Romans, and the emperor Theodosius I. cancelled the Games because he considered them pagan festivals that offended Christian religious doctrines. The tracks and arenas of Olympia soon fell into ruins, and the natural crumbling and decay caused by the passing of time were made worse by two violent earthquakes. The excitement and the glory of the games were forgotten until the last century (1875) when the ruins of Olympia were uncovered by archaeologists.

Revival of the Games

The discovery of the ancient site aroused great interest in the Olympic Games among scholars. They studied the odes of Pindar in a new light, and they closely examined the paintings of competing athletes on ancient Greek jars and vases.

The idea of drawing together athletes from many areas to compete in a spirit of mutual support and good sportsmanship has a timeless appeal. Baron Pierre de Coubertin, a French nobleman, was so inspired by the ideals of the ancient games that he worked tirelessly to convince the nations of the world to create a modern series of athletic contests. Thanks to him, the Olympic Games were resumed in 1896.

The first site of the new games was Athens (in honor of the first Olympians), and since then international competitions have been held every four years in different cities throughout the world. In the future, however, the games will be staggered, with the winter sports taking place one year and the summer sports taking place two years later. Therefore, an Olympiad will be two rather than four years long.

Many of the traditions of the ancient Olympics have survived. For example, just as in early times an athlete lit a fire at the altar of Zeus to mark the beginning of the festival, a modern runner carries a torch and ignites the fire that burns throughout the period the Games take place in the host city. And the Greek tradition of fair play continues to inspire the athletes of the modern world.

Questions:

1. Where is Olympia?
2. Why did the first Olympic Games take place?
3. Describe the stadium at Olympia.
4. What was the pancratium?
5. Describe the racing events at the games.
6. What cultural events took place at the games?
7. What was the highest honor an Olympian athlete could win?
8. How were the victors honored in their cities?
9. What are some other games that took place in ancient Greece?
10. How do the modern Olympics maintain the old traditions of the early Greeks?

Ideas to Think About

1. There is a famous story about Callipatira, the mother of an athlete in ancient Greece who was determined to see her son compete. Since women were not allowed in Olympia during the events, she disguised herself as a man! Unfortunately, she was found out as she enthusiastically cheered her son on, but the officials were lenient. They understood her great pride in her son's athletic accomplishments, and so she was not punished.

2. A huge forty-foot high ivory and gold statue of Zeus created by the Greek sculptor Phidias once dominated the temple at Olympia. Its great beauty made it one of the seven wonders of the ancient world. Unfortunately, it disappeared long ago and we only know of its existence and appearance through ancient writings.

3. As we have learned, the Olympic Games were held every four years regardless of war or natural catastrophe. Unfortunately, the Persians did not honor the Greek tradition of calling off all battles during the time of the competitions. Thus, while Leonidas stood firm at Thermopylae, thousands of Greek citizens were watching Theagenes of Thasas win the pancratium!

4. The events of the Olympic Games tell us a lot about the daily lives of the ancient Greeks. The great distances between the city-states required men to become strong runners in order to carry messages from one city to another. The many brooks and streams that flow down the hillsides encouraged the young men to jump a relatively long distance, or else land in the water! (Greek pastures were not surrounded by fences, so athletes did not consider high jumping.) Of course, the spear was an essential weapon of the Greek soldier, and once he lost it, he might resort to throwing stones before he engaged in hand-to-hand combat. The skills required of young Greeks are clearly reflected in the foot race, broad jump, javelin throw, discus throw, and wrestling (and boxing) matches included in the athletic games.

5. Winning at Olympia brought great glory to the polis of the victor. Solon once offered five hundred drachmas (a great amount in those days) to any Athenian who won an olive wreath. When runner Leonidas of Rhodes won three events in each of four successive games, earning a record number of twelve olive wreaths, the people of Rhodes declared him a god!

Projects:

1. One of the events of the modern Olympic Games is the pentathalon. Find out what this is and present a short report to the class.

2. Organize some athletic events for your class based on the original Olympic Games. Contestants can use frisbees as discuses and carry garbage can lids in the hoplite race. Use your imagination to plan other events, but do not include boxing or the pancratium! Write an oath of sportsmanship to be recited by the contestants at the beginning of the "games," and make some wreaths from the branches of a bush (forsythia makes excellent wreaths!) for the winners.

3. Do a research project on the Olympic Games of the twentieth century, showing their similarities to and differences from the original games. Who are some of the famous champions?

4. Some historians say that the Olympic Games developed from funeral games held in memory of the Greek hero Pelops. Find out about the story of Pelops' chariot race (if you haven't already done so!), and write a short report. Look in a book about Greek myths for your data.

5. Explain the meaning and derivation of the modern expression "resting on one's laurels." Give three examples.

Chapter XII — THE GOLDEN AGE

A New Alliance

Although the Persians no longer seemed an imminent threat, the Greeks could not be certain that they would not attack again in the future. The unified front presented by the city-states during the Persian Wars had been the key to their victory against the invaders, and many Greeks believed that it was important to form a permanent alliance. Therefore, the Athenians led a movement to organize a group of city-states into a confederation. The cities located on the Aegean islands and in Ionia were quick to join, because they feared that they were easy prey for Persian warships. Each city in the confederation was asked to contribute either ships or a sum of money to build up a fleet that would patrol the extensive Greek coast-line and protect its citizens from an enemy assault. Athens immediately offered her entire fleet of two hundred triremes.

The money collected was kept on Delos, an Aegean island sacred to Apollo (it was supposedly his birthplace), and for this reason the organization became known as the Delian League. It had eventually over two hundred member cities. To seal the alliance, the members dramatically hurled iron weights into the sea; this act symbolized their determination to support each other "until the iron floated to the surface." The Athenians assumed the leadership of the organization from the start.

The Spartans had no interest in joining the League and remained the dominant power in the Peloponnese. We will learn more about them in the next chapter.

A Transformation

The Delian League functioned effectively for a long time. The fleet grew large, and the isolated city-states of the Aegean were well protected. After twelve years the Greeks no longer feared the Persians, but when two member city-states (on the islands of Euboea and Samos) tried to withdraw from the League they were attacked by the Athenian fleet and bullied into submission. This made many of the other members understandably uncomfortable. And the Athenians exerted their authority in other ways as well. They claimed final jurisdiction over all court cases held in the League; furthermore, they demanded that all member cities use Athenian coins as well as the Athenian system of weights and measures. Finally, they ordered every city in the League to adopt a democratic government based upon the Athenian model.

In 454 B.C. the treasury was moved from Delos to Athens (supposedly for safe-guarding). Before long, some of the money was being diverted for the rebuilding of major parts of that city (remember how it had been destroyed by the Persians?). Such unauthorized use of funds caused bitter resentment among the League members, but they felt powerless to do anything about it.

Although most of the economic measures imposed by the Athenians were beneficial to all members of the League, domination by a central power went counter to the centuries-long Greek tradition of independence and self-government. Many a citizen living in the Aegean basin must have shuddered as he realized that the Delian League had now evolved into the Athenian Empire!

A Great Prosperity

But apart from the grumbling among many of the city-states about Athens' chain-rattling, most of Greece was enjoying the benefits of peace and prosperity. Freed from the fear of foreign invasion, the people were able to devote their time and energy to practical pursuits. The Greek fleet basically eliminated the danger of pirates, and trade between mainland Greece and the rest of the Mediterranean world continued to expand.

The fifth century B.C. was to be the high point in the development of politics, imaginative writing, and art in the civilization of ancient Greece. This blossoming of Greek culture was centered, of course, in Athens. It is known as the Golden Age; it is also referred to as the (early) Classical Period of Greek civilization.

Democracy

As we have seen, the seeds of democracy were sown in very early times, and a way of life that respected individual liberties evolved in Athens during the centuries following the Dorian invasion. By 500 B.C. the Athenian government was neatly organized into three distinct branches: one dealt with the making of laws (the legislative branch), another was responsible for the interpretation of those laws when conflicts arose among the citizens (the judicial branch), and a third focused upon the enforcement of the laws (the executive branch). Many of the other Greek city-states adopted a democratic form of government (of course, League members were ordered to do so), but the system worked most effectively in Athens, and so it is Athenian democracy that we will study here.

The Legislative Branch

During the Golden Age the Ecclesia (the general assembly of citizens) met on a hillside just below the Acropolis called the Pnyx about once every ten days. All male citizens were expected to attend, but remember that only free adult male Greeks possessing a certain income were citizens; out of a population of 150,000, only about 40,000 met these qualifications.

At least six thousand citizens had to be present for a meeting of the Ecclesia to take place. Sometimes, when there were no burning issues to discuss, only a small number of men showed up at the Pnyx. On these occasions, a quorum of citizens (the minimum number necessary to start the meeting) was herded up by special government officials using ropes dyed with wet red paint; if a citizen managed to slip out from the rope but picked up the tell-tale red stain on his clothing, he would be fined for non-attendance!

Every meeting opened with a prayer followed by the sacrifice of a pig to the gods. Then the discussion of public matters began. Any Athenian citizen could propose a new law or speak for (or against) someone else's proposal. Although only a fraction of the citizens attended a given meeting, and the citizens represented only a fraction of the total population of Athens, the Ecclesia was the closest thing to true democracy the world had ever known.

Every year, five hundred citizens were chosen by lot (at random) among the membership of the Ecclesia. These men made up the Boule, a council of five hundred (increased from Solon's four hundred—see page 67). They handled the day-to-day running of the city. They also drew up a list of matters to be discussed by the Ecclesia, such as building and road repairs, the payment of city workers, and whether or not the city should go to war. Since no one could be on the Boule more than twice, the positions were passed around to a large number of men. Eventually, almost every Athenian citizen who regularly attended the Ecclesia meetings had a chance to serve on the Boule.

The Judicial Branch

The judicial branch of government dealt with legal matters. Whenever a crime was committed, a jury was chosen (again by lot) among the members of the Ecclesia. (The old Areopagus was now defunct.) All citizens over thirty were expected to volunteer for this duty. There were no judges, nor were there lawyers to represent clients.

The accused person addressed the jury and pleaded his case himself (although a timid man was free to have a friend speak on his behalf). The Greeks considered public speaking an important skill, and at times like this a persuasive argument could determine the future of a man's life! The accused was allowed only six minutes to plead his case; the time was measured by *clepsydra* ("water-stealers"), a pair of clay pots set so that water dripped from one to the other in exactly six minutes. Then the jury (which could number from 101 to 1001 men!) voted to determine the defendant's guilt or innocence. Every juror was given two wheel-shaped bronze tokens; the token with a solid center was used to indicate innocence, while one with a hollow center pronounced guilt. At the end of a trial, the juror selected one of the two tokens and dropped it into a clay jar. Then the "votes" were counted. Should the accused be found guilty, the jury voted on the appropriate punishment.

The Executive Branch

An elite group of men known as the Ten Generals (the *Strategoi*) headed the Athenian government. They were elected annually by the Ecclesia and could serve an unlimited number of terms. They selected among themselves a Commander-in-chief who thereby became the very highest government official (like a president). The Ten Generals met every day and carried out the policies decided upon by the Boule and the Ecclesia; they also met with foreign envoys, discussed economic issues, supervised government officials such as tax collectors, and, if necessary, declared war. Occasionally, the Commander-in-chief delivered a speech to the public.

Executive Branch	Legislative Branch	Judicial Branch
The Commander-in-chief	The Boule	The Public Jury
The Strategoi	The Ecclesia	

fig. 61 — **The three branches of Greek government**

Ostracism

Years earlier, the archon Cleisthenes had devised an ingenious way to deal with those government leaders who seemed a threat to Greek democracy. The Greeks had a strong penchant for order and harmony, and the words "nothing in excess" that had been carved on the walls at Delphi clearly reflected their adherence to moderation in all matters. Thus, when a leader appeared inordinate in his demands or seemed to be "rocking the ship of state," a citizen could simply write the name of the offender on a piece of broken pottery (an *ostracon)* and drop it into a large container near the Pynx. Special meetings were held during which the ostraca were ceremoniously deposited; then they were retrieved by government officials. If the number of ostraca reached six thousand, the man whose name was written the most times was banished (ostracized) from the city for ten years. After that period of time, he could return to Athens as though nothing had happened! Today, the word ostracize means "to exclude a person from a group or society."

Fortunately, in the seventy years that this system was used, only ten men suffered the unpleasant fate of ostracism. Hundreds of ostraca have been found in archaeological excavations. Surprisingly enough, the names of some of the greatest leaders of the Golden Age were written upon these pottery fragments. Even then, no one could please all the people all the time!

Pericles

About twenty years after the Persian Wars ended, the Strategoi selected as Commander-in-Chief a man of out-standing ability who would leave his mark upon their city. This was Pericles, a statesman, orator (public speaker) and military leader. He was the great nephew of Cleisthenes, and he governed for over thirty years (460-429 B.C.). Pericles was annually elected during that period by the Ecclesia, and

fig. 62 — **Statue of Pericles**

so his power came directly from the people; yet, his brilliance, charisma and sense of vision enabled him to personally mold the major policies of Athens during the three decades he was in power.

Pericles was proud of Athens' rich heritage, and he believed that the city should set a shining example for the rest of Greece. During his terms of office, many brilliant artists, writers, and scientists were attracted to what was rapidly becoming the intellectual and creative center of the Greek world.

Pericles loosened some of the financial requirements for citizenship and saw to it that those who served in government were paid for their services. Now a merchant could afford to serve at court or attend a meeting of the Ecclesia or the Boule without sacrificing any of his income. As a result, official policies were no longer based solely upon the interests of the wealthy elite. Athens could proudly boast that every citizen was the master of his own person and an active participant in his city's government.

A Corridor to the Sea

One of Pericles' first goals was to fortify Athens against foreign invasion. A long wooden palisade already encircled the Acropolis (remember the wooden walls?) and a twenty-foot high stone wall surrounded the entire city. But Athens lay five miles inland from the sea, and Pericles worried that an enemy could easily surround and besiege the city, cutting off the food supply. After carefully studying the local landscape, he ordered the construction of two long stone walls (about five hundred feet apart) stretching from Athens to the harbor of Piraeus. The walls would provide a safe corridor through which food could be delivered from ships moored at Piraeus. Since the Athenian fleet ruled the high seas, the corridor seemed to insure Athens' survival in the most trying of circumstances.

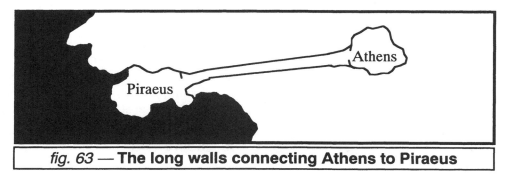

fig. 63 — **The long walls connecting Athens to Piraeus**

Once the city seemed secure, Pericles turned his attention to the buildings themselves. After the Persians sacked and burned Athens, new structures of mud-brick had been built on the site. But Pericles envisioned something considerably grander, and it was he who quietly withdrew some of the Delian funds to hire the best artists and architects in Greece. Under his guidance, plans were made for the construction of elegant marble temples, majestic government buildings, and graceful colonnades around the agora (marketplace).

The Acropolis

The Athenian Acropolis, once the site of a Mycenean citadel, rose dramatically 260 feet above the city. Since Dorian days it had been the spiritual center of Athens, the site of several temples dedicated to the city's patron goddess, Athena. Pericles decided that the time was right to level everything left standing on the hilltop in order to construct the finest temples the people of the ancient world had ever seen. The temples would lavishly honor Athena, and the Acropolis would become an

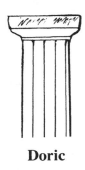
Doric

Ionic

Corinthian

The basic concept of columns possibly came from Egypt, where beautiful stone pillars had been used for millennia. There are many styles of Greek column; they differ mainly in the design of the capital (the top section). The Doric column has a simple capital which reflects the primitive, down-to-earth Dorian culture. It was the most popular type of column in mainland Greece. The graceful Ionic column came from the artistic people of Ionia and was popular there and on the Aegean Islands. Its capital appears to be framed with a set of curled ram's horns. The elaborate Corinthian column became popular after the Golden Age, and it seems to convey the somewhat ostentatious nature of the merchants of Corinth. Its capital is decorated with acanthus leaves. It was not used very often in ancient Greece, but later it became very popular with the Romans.

fig. 64 — **Three types of columns**

awe-inspiring symbol of the city's power and greatness.

As we have learned, the design of a typical Greek temple was simple yet elegant. Its rectangular structure was surrounded by tall graceful pillars that supported a pitched roof and formed a colonnade (columned porch) around the outer edges of the building. The triangular gables at the front and back of the building were called pediments. A temple's entrance always faced east, so that the rays of the morning sun could fall upon the statue of the god or goddess that stood in the inner sanctuary.

The Parthenon

The most impressive temple built on the Acropolis was the Parthenon (it derives its name from *Athena Parthenos*, which means "Athena the Maiden.") Pericles commissioned the architects Ictinus and Callicrates to design the building, and its actual construction required fourteen years.

Today the ruins of the Parthenon still dominate the hilltop above the modern bustling city of Athens. Its very dimensions are imposing: It is 228 feet long, 101 feet wide and 65 feet high. Originally the building had a wooden roof covered with clay tiles, but this was destroyed in the seventeenth century. Fluted Doric columns once supported the roof. Seventeen columns flank each side of the building, while eight extend across the front and rear walls. The vertical lines of fluting cut into the stone trap long shadows, which make the columns appear slender and graceful. The Greeks understood how the physical world can play tricks on the human eye, creating an optical illusion. For this reason, the architects designed columns that bulge in the center, taper at the top and lean slightly inward. Had the columns been built perfectly straight, they would have appeared to be leaning outward from their bases; given their actual design, they look straight and tall when viewed from a distance. There is no trace of the paint that once embellished the columns, but the white marble contains veins of iron that give the building a golden glow at dawn and dusk.

The wide marble steps leading up to the front of the Parthenon are higher

*fig. 65 — **The Parthenon***

in the center than they are on the sides. Here again, the architects compensated for the effects of an optical illusion. If the wide steps were completely level, a person observing from a distance would have thought that the entire temple and its stairway sagged dramatically in the middle!

The temple is decorated with relief figures (cut into a stone background) and free-standing sculptures that were designed and carved by Phidias, the very same man who created the giant statue of Zeus in Olympia (see page 114 #2); however, given the tremendous number of figures adorning the temple, we must assume that Phidias had several assistants working with him on the project.

A band of carved marble runs along the top of the outer walls of the temple. This is called a frieze; it is 520 feet long and a little more than three feet high. The carvings depict a procession of young Athenian men, some on horse-back and others leading sheep and cows to be sacrificed to Athena at the concluding ceremonies of the Panathenaic Games. Also represented in the procession are maidens and government magistrates, and in one section there is a group of seated Olympian gods who seem to be viewing the parading figures with great interest.

fig. 66— **The seated gods**

The triangular pediments on the front and rear gables of the temple are decorated with free-standing sculptures. Unfortunately, many of the statues have disappeared, but descriptions of them that were written centuries ago give us an idea of what they must have looked like in the days of Pericles. Those figures over the main entrance represented the birth of Athena (remember that Athena sprang fully armed from the head of Zeus). The sculptures on the rear pediment portray the contest between Athena and Poseidon (each wanted to be the patron deity of Athens). According to Greek myth, Poseidon thrust his trident into a rock and water flowed down to the sea; he then promised to bring the city riches through sea trade if he was chosen patron god. (In another version of the myth he offered the horse.) Athena's offering was an olive tree. The people of the city considered the olive tree more useful than Poseidon's water, and so they made Athena their patron goddess.

Religious ceremonies for the general public were held at altars placed outside the temple. The interior of the building was the home of the deity, and it was reserved for private prayers by priests and privileged citizens. Originally, a majestic forty-foot high statue of Athena, sculpted by Phidias in gold and ivory around a wooden core, stood in one of the two inner chambers of the Parthenon; the crown upon her head nearly brushed the ceiling. Phidias carefully designed the statue so that the gold plating could be removed and weighed in order to prove that he had used every ounce of gold delivered to him. Even then, the government officials were suspicious of their employees! This magnificent statue disappeared centuries ago (it was carried off to Constantinople and later destroyed in a fire), but we know of its existence because it is carefully described in the works of Greek historians.

A detailed guidebook written by Pausanias, a Greek traveler of the second century A.D. (the same man who described the Mycenean grave-stones—see page 52), enabled modern archaeologists to discover the actual studio of Phidias. Among the ruins of the workshop lay many of the tools and terra-cotta molds once used by that great artist.

Other Temples on the Acropolis

The Acropolis was also the site of several smaller temples of great beauty. The Erechtheum was built on the north side of the hilltop. It was named for Erechtheus, a legendary ancestor of the city's Mycenean kings. Its columns are of the Ionic style. On the south side of the temple is the small Porch of the Maidens; the roof is supported by Caryatids (carved stone female figures) instead of traditional columns.

A small temple dedicated to Athena Nike (*nike* means "victorious") was built to commemorate the Greek victory over the Persians. The frieze on the outer walls depicts one of the battles of the Persian Wars.

The Propylaea is a ceremonial gateway to the Acropolis. It is a

fig. 67
A Caryatid

curious mixture of Doric and Ionic marble columns; the stone dramatically changes color throughout the day, varying from gold and honey in the early hours to rose and gray toward dusk. Not far from the Propylaea was a huge bronze statue of Athena: The crest of her helmet and the point of her spear could be seen by sailors entering the distant harbor at Pireaus.

Advances in Sculpture

The sculptures of the temples of the Acropolis give us an idea of the great advances made by the Greek artists since the Archaic period. While the earlier figures were stiff and unnatural, those of the Golden Age are extremely life-like representations of handsome men and women. These statues are remarkable for their beauty and grace as well as the feeling of quiet restraint that they convey. And they bear witness to the genius of the Greeks, who could create harmony and order out of a formless block of stone—just as Gaea and Uranus had once molded Cosmos out of Chaos.

An excellent example of Golden Age sculpture is the statue of Heracles (see fig. 68). Another well-known work of the fifth century is "the Discus Thrower" by Myron: This bronze statue captures a moment in

fig. 68 — **Heracles**
Francis Bartlett Donation of 1912 — Courtesy, Museum of Fine Arts, Boston

time when a young athlete, his muscles straining, turns and prepares to throw a weighted discus. His powerful body is controlled and restrained as he makes his move. Although the original statue has disappeared, many copies of it have been found.

Another gifted sculptor of the Golden Age was Polyclitus, an artist with a knack for mathematics. He worked out a mathematical formula for the physical dimensions of a statue: The figure was divided into seven sections, each equal to the size of its head. These were further subdivided into sections the size of a palm. For example, the lower leg from the foot to the kneecap was three palms. His precise formula was followed by most classical sculptors who came after him.

Greek statues were used to decorate not only temples but private homes as well. They were also made to commemorate the lives of famous people and to mark graves. Although most of the statues have disappeared, a fair number have survived for us to appreciate. Many broken works of art have been recovered from the soil of the Acropolis itself. Others have been discovered at the bottom of the sea, often aboard ancient sunken mer-

chant ships that capsized in storms. A beautiful bronze statue of Poseidon (some say Zeus) was found beneath the waters of the Aegean. This seems an appropriate place to find Poseidon since he was the god of the sea! Fortunately, the Roman artists were so

fig. 69 — **Attic Black Figure Neck Amphora**
Gift of Thomas G. Appleton, Courtesy, Museum of Fine Arts, Boston

impressed with the Greek sculptures that they made numerous copies of them, and, like the Discus Thrower, many of these have often survived the ravages of time when the Greek originals have not.

Pottery

The clay vases and jugs molded by Greek potters are an important source of information about life in those early times. Vessels of many shapes and sizes are decorated with paintings of Olympic athletes, the heroes and monsters of Homer's epics, and scenes of everyday Athenian life. The vases made during the sixth century B.C. have black figures against a red background (see fig. 69), while those of the fifth century are the reverse (red figures against a black background). The coloration of the pottery depends upon the method by which it was fired.

There was a particular district in Athens where the potters had their workshops. It was called Ceramicus, and this is the source of our word "ceramics".

Drama

One of the most important achievements of the Golden Age was in drama. Theater as we know it was invented by the Greeks, and the art of playwriting blossomed in the fifth century. The earliest plays grew out of impromptu forms of entertainment at religious festivals. The Festival of Dionysus was held each

fig. 70 — **Attic Red Figure**
Catharine Page Perkins Fund, Courtesy Museum of Fine Arts, Boston

spring in Athens to mark the budding of the leaves of the grapevine (sacred to the wine god). During the festivities, local men donned goatskins and dressed as satyrs (mythical creatures, half man and half goat). They gaily danced around a statue of Dionysus, while a chorus sang about the exploits and achievements of the god to the accompaniment of a double flute and drum. From this simple beginning, Greek tragic drama slowly evolved into a sophisticated art form. Actually, the word tragedy comes from the Greek word *tragoedia* meaning "goat song".

Tradition credits the poet Thespis (from the island of Icaria) with first providing lines for a single member of the chorus to recite in response to those of the rest of the group. Today, the word thespian means "actor." Eventually, other writers produced plays in which two or three soloists conversed among themselves, and the role of the chorus was gradually reduced to simply providing background information about the actions being portrayed or discussed by the soloists. Music was an important part of a theatrical performance, and many lines were sung to the accompaniment of a flute.

The Great Playwrights

The tragedies that were written during the Golden Age often dealt with the rather strained relations between human beings and the Olympic gods and goddesses, and they focused upon the difficulties of trying to lead a good life.

Aeschylus (525-456 B.C.) was the first of three great playwrights of the Golden Age. He had been a soldier at Marathon and Salamis, and as a young man he wrote a play entitled THE PERSIANS (his producer was the young Pericles himself!). His later works are based upon Greek myths and legends, and they deal with the agony experienced by an individual caught in a conflict. THE ORESTIA is a trilogy about three generations of the family of King Agamemnon of Mycenae.

The greatest tragic playwright was Sophocles (496-406 B.C.). His name means "the wise and honored one." Like many Greek scholars, he was intrigued by the complexity of the human mind. He once said that the world is full of wonders, but nothing is more wonderful than man. Yet, man has his faults. Sophocles observed that a superabundance of one trait, such as envy or pride (the much dreaded *hubris*), upset a natural balance and caused a person's downfall. The prophetic words, "Nothing in excess," inscribed on the wall of Apollo's temple long before, remained the motto of every educated Greek, and those who ignored this call for restraint were "out of sync" with the ideals of classical society.

The plays of Sophocles depict people who are victimized by a lack of balance in their characters or in their lives; they struggle valiantly but hopelessly against forces that are greater than themselves. Sophocles wrote 113 plays, but only seven have survived. Two of his most popular works are ANTIGONE and OEDIPUS THE KING.

The works of Euripides (480-406 B.C.), the last of the "big three" of Athens, often concern a person who brings ruin upon himself (and usually his family as well) because he allows his emotions to master his powers of reason. His most powerful play, MEDEA, is based upon the story of Jason and the Golden Fleece.

It has been said that while Sophocles saw men as they ought to be (his main characters are heroic), Euripides saw men as they actually are. Euripides was openly critical of the traditional Greek religion, and he described the long-worshiped Olympian gods as cruel, deceitful and immoral beings who were not worthy of respect.

In the Comic Vein

Greek comedies were light-hearted, often irreverent plays that poked fun at human weaknesses and mocked many aspects of everyday life and politics. Often the names of people sitting in the audience—even generals and statesmen—were included in a frolicsome episode. The greatest of the comic poets was Aristophanes (445-385 B.C.)

An On-going Tradition

Thousands of plays (comedies and tragedies) were written by the ancient Greeks. Although most of them have been lost, thirty-three have survived relatively intact, and these are still produced and enjoyed by modern audiences. The intricacy of the human soul and the difficulties that arise when individuals are brought into conflict with each other or with the fates are timeless subjects that will always intrigue the minds of thoughtful people.

The Theater

The Greeks invented the open air theater for the production of their plays. After the temples of the Acropolis had been rebuilt, Pericles ordered the construction of the huge theater of Dionysus on the south slope of the famous hilltop. (Dionysus thus became the god of the theater as well as the divinity of wine!)

The stone seats of the amphitheater were arranged in a semi-circle; they accommodated 18,000 people. The front rows were reserved for the priests of Dionysus, government officials, and other guests of honor. At the bottom of the slope was a circular area (called the *orchestra*) where the chorus stood. Beyond the orchestra was a raised stage (the *proscenium*). Behind it was a long building (the *skene*) which served as a dressing room. The wall of the skene facing the audience could be decorated as a background for the play being presented on the stage. This is the origin of our word "scene".

Behind the skene was a crane with pulley and weights. It was used to transport an actor through the air when he was playing the role of a god or goddess! This device was called a *mechane* (machine); the Romans later called the sudden appearance of a deity by this means *deus ex machina* ("a god transported by the machine"). The Latin phrase is still used today to describe an artificial or miraculous event written into a play to solve a thorny problem in the plot.

The Greeks also had some other ingenious special effects. For example, they created the sound of thunder by propelling large round rocks through a tunnel built under the seats of the audience. The thunder claps must have

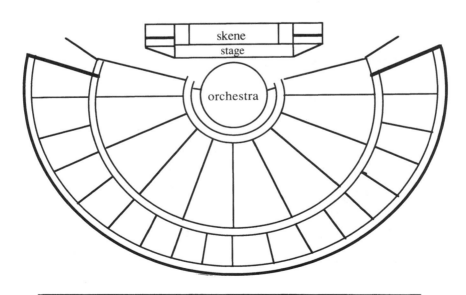

fig. 71 — **A Greek amphitheater**

been startling to those sitting just above the tunnel!

The acoustics (transport of sound waves) of the open-air theaters were remarkably effective. At the ancient theater of Epidaurus, the voice of a person standing on the stage can be clearly heard in the very last row. This restored theater is currently used for annual drama festivals.

The performers of the Golden Age were professional actors who were paid by the state. Men played the male as well as female parts, since women were not allowed to participate in theatricals. The actors were held in high esteem by the people, and they were even exempt from military service. The Greek word for actor is *hypocrites*, and our word hypocrite is derived from it. Like an actor, a hypocrite pretends to be something that he isn't!

The Greek actors wore padded clothes and ten-inch platform shoes to make them appear "larger than life." They also wore masks made of stiffened linen, the mouths of which were shaped like megaphones to

fig. 72 — **Theatrical masks**

amplify their voices. The facial expression of a mask worn for a tragedy was sorrowful, while a comic mask had a laughing face. Special masks were worn to represent female characters.

Going to the theater in Athens was an all-day affair, since many plays (usually three tragedies and a comedy) were presented together at a single performance. The plays at the Festival of Dionysus were presented over a period of three days. A theater-goer took along a box lunch to consume during an interval between plays; he also probably carried along a soft pillow to sit upon (remember, the seats were of stone!). During such a festival all business was suspended, law courts were closed, and prisoners were even released from their cells! Tickets to the plays were inexpensive, and those people who could not afford them had their way paid by the state, since theater-going was considered a civic as well as a religious activity. What better way was there to celebrate Greece's cultural heritage?

Since the plays were based upon well-known myths and legends, everyone in the audience knew the gist of the stories. What interested the crowd was the manner in which a play was presented. The audience openly displayed approval or disapproval of a production by stamping their feet, shouting at the actors, or cheering boisterously. Occasionally they threw rocks and vegetables to indicate their displeasure!

In earliest times the writer of the best tragic trilogy was given a goat, while the best comedy won its author a jug of wine and a basket of figs. By the Golden Age, the prizes were usually a Dionysian wreath of grapevine or a sum of money; they were awarded at the end of the performances to the best producer, the best actor, and the best playwright. Sophocles won first prize at the festival twenty times!

The Poets

Music and poetry were closely related. The poets of the late Archaic Age had broken with the heroic tradition of Homer and begun to write about themselves—their loves, their sorrows and their hopes. Following in this tradition of self-expression, the poets of the Golden Age wrote many beautiful and evocative descriptions of basic human emotions. Because these works were recited or chanted to the accompaniment of a lyre (a small harp), they are called lyric poetry. Today, we use this term to describe expressive poems dealing with human emotional experiences. Men called rhapsodes often recited poetry (rhapsodies) at religious festivals.

The First Historian

We have already heard a great deal about Herodotus, the Father of History. He was born in Halicarnasus (just south of Ionia) in 485 B.C. Like most of the Greeks of his time, Herodotus was extremely curious about the nature of the world. He asked many questions and thoroughly investigated matters that he didn't understand. As a young man he traveled widely, visiting Egypt, Phoenicia and Babylon and taking copious notes about the customs and historical events of the local areas. Unlike Homer, Herodotus dealt only with the real and the factual. Yet, he wasn't the first Greek to look beyond the mythological explanations of life posed by his ancestors. In the sixth century B.C. Hecataeus of Miletus had tried to describe as accurately as possible the events of the past; he once remarked, "the stories of the Greeks (of earlier centuries) are numerous, and, in my opinion, ridiculous!"

Herodotus carefully studied the geography of the lands he visited, for he believed that the natural environment strongly influenced the development of a culture. On his visit to Egypt, for example, he ascended the Nile

River to the First Cataract (a series of rapids) and wrote a detailed description of the landscape.

Herodotus later settled in Athens, where he wrote his great work THE HISTORY (the Greek word *historia* means "an inquiry"). This massive volume is a thoughtful study of Greek civilization, centering upon the period of the Persian Wars. It also includes a scholarly analysis of the rise of the Persian empire, a colorful description of the contrasting cultures of Athens and Sparta, and a lively commentary on the customs of the Egyptians and the Scythians (people living in western Asia).

THE HISTORY is the oldest surviving study of its kind, and as such it is an invaluable source of data relating to the ancient world. Although he was frequently so caught up by his enthusiasm for his subject that he exaggerated many of his descriptions, Herodotus was the first scholar to separate history from legend, basing his writings (generally speaking) upon established facts. In the opening lines of his work, he wrote of the importance of making a record of the times "so that past deeds will not be forgotten through the lapse of time." Thanks to him, our knowledge of those past deeds is greater than it would otherwise have been.

A Prolific Time

The Golden Age of Athens must have been an exhilarating time to live. Imagine being a witness to the explosion of creativity that had been building up for so many centuries! Indeed, over a period of only eighty years, a relative handful of men achieved more in a wider variety of fields than any other society has ever done in a similar space of time.

Questions:

1. What was the original purpose of the Delian League?
2. Why did many of the members of the League begin to resent Athens?
3. What were the qualifications for citizenship?
4. What were the three branches of the Greek government?
5. What is ostracism?
6. Why did Pericles build a wall?
7. Describe the frieze of the Parthenon.
8. How did Greek drama originate?
9. Describe a Greek theater.
10. What are the strengths and weaknesses of Herodotus' works?

Ideas To Think About:

1. The island of Delos, sacred to Apollo (it was his birthplace), was so hallowed that no one was allowed to be born or to die there. Therefore, all pregnant

women and sick people were taken across a narrow channel to another island, Rhenea.

2. Themistocles, the hero of the Battle of Salamis during the Persian Wars, oversaw the building of the walls of Athens. In 471 B.C. he was ostracized, and so he settled in the city of Argos. He was later accused of treason (he apparently spoke against the alliance with Sparta and was too closely associated with the Persians). And so he moved on, this time to Anatolia, where the Persian King Artaxerxes (who was grateful to him for helping to negotiate peace with Athens after the war) made him governor of three cities. Themistocles lived well until he was sixty-five. Some scholars believe he then ended his own life. (Did he pine for his homeland?)

3. The olive tree, sacred to Athena and the symbol of her city, was a source of Athenian commercial wealth. It is a stately tree with a thick grey trunk and lovely green leaves whose silver backs are revealed in a gentle breeze. It requires sixteen years to mature and forty years to reach its peak production of fruit. This being so, it is not surprising that Pericles declared it a criminal offense to uproot or cut down an olive tree!

4. The Parthenon survived relatively intact for nearly two thousand years. When Athena was no longer worshiped, the building was used as a Christian church and, more recently, as a Moslem mosque. The Turks later made the temple a storehouse for gunpowder. In 1687 Italian soldiers besieged some Turks who were quartered on the Acropolis; the Italians threw a grenade-like device that exploded and destroyed the inside structures of the ancient temple as well as the roof. An earthquake in a later century further contributed to the crumbling of some of the outer walls. It is a tragedy that an insignificant battle in modern times could substantially damage a magnificent building that had endured nearly intact for centuries.

5. A Roman historian named Vetruvius wrote that the Caryatids fought with the Persians at the battle of Salamis against the Greeks. After the Greeks won the battle, they destroyed the city of the Caryatids. They killed all the men and brought the women back to Athens as slaves. Greek sculptors copied the Caryatid slave women in stone, forcing them to carry the roof of the Erectheum on their heads for eternity. Today, a column in the shape of a woman is called a caryatid, while one depicting a man is an atlas.

6. In the last century, Lord Elgin of Great Britain "rescued" parts of a frieze of the Parthenon, sculptures from the pediment, and one of the Caryatids of the porch of the Erectheum. They are now in the British Museum and are referred to as the Elgin Marbles. Many people feel that they should be returned to Athens. Indeed, it is now a law that any artifacts discovered on Greek soil must be given to local authorities and displayed in Greek museums.

7. Although their tragedies often contain references to violent acts, the Greeks considered it inappropriate to have these acts take place upon the stage. For this reason, characters were always wounded or murdered off-stage. The audience would simply hear the screams of the victim! There were two doors at the middle of the wall of the skene. After an offstage murder, the doors would open and a platform on wheels (an *eccyclema*) carried out the draped body of "the deceased" for the audience to see!

Projects:

1. The division of our government into three branches (legislative, executive and judicial) has its origins in the democracy of ancient Athens. Find out more about the functions of the three branches in American government; then compare and contrast them with their counterparts in Athens. Using poster board, make a chart comparing the two systems of government.

2. Greek architectural styles are evident throughout our country. Look at the buildings in your city. Pay particular attention to government buildings and stately mansions. What kinds of pillars do you see (Doric, Ionic or Corinthian)? Look through magazines and clip pictures of buildings that show a Greek influence. Make a collage of the pictures.

3. Sappho was a Greek poetess from the island of Lesbos. Her poignant odes and poems reflect her ideas about such human emotions as love and friendship. Find out more about her and her works. Present a report to the class. Quote a few lines from her poems, if possible.

4. A Greek slave named Aesop is credited with the creation of many fables that are read to this very day. These include the stories of the tortoise and the hare and the fox and the crow. Read a collection of Aesop's fables and make a report to the class.

5. Read a tragedy by Aeschylus, Sophocles or Euripides and a comedy by Aristophanes. Write a short report explaining why these plays, written so long ago, have a strong appeal for modern audiences.

6. Here is how a Greek artist made a mask for the theater: He put olive oil on the face of the actor, then lay narrow strips of linen around his head, leaving openings for his eyes, nostrils and mouth; then other strips were dipped in a paste made from flour and water and placed criss-cross over the first ones; after about ten minutes, he cut through the strips at the back of the actor's head and removed it. He could then build up the nose and other facial features by adding more linen and then smoothing it over with plaster. After the mask dried, he painted it and then coated it with a substance like varnish.

You can make your own mask with your teacher following these steps, but with some variations. Using a combination of strips of bandage or paper and glue made from flour and water, shape your mask on the face of a friend or else over the outside of a glass bowl. Remove it, and when it is dry, decorate it. Use the mask to put on an original play.

7. Below is a photo of a famous Greek statue (at least part of it!). Doesn't it look real? Isn't it amazing that a sculptor could make a piece of stone look like folds of cloth? Next time you visit a large city museum, go to the area devoted to classical statues and see if you can find works of art similar to this one.

fig. 73 — **Cybele**
H. L. Pierce Fund, Courtesy Museum of Fine Arts, Boston

Chapter XIII — SPARTA CLINGS TO THE PAST

Unlike Athens, Sparta remained a stronghold of the military ways of Dorian times. Any spirit of creativity and experimentation had been permanently stifled after the rebellion of the Messenians (see page 64).

Sparta's close-minded government stood in stark contrast to those of the democratic city-states. It was a monarchy, although two kings rather than one ruled at a given time. The duties of the two rulers were simple; they commanded the army in times of war and they conducted religious ceremonies. In all other matters, the government was run by a group of five overseers (called the *Ephors*) who were elected annually. A Council of Elders made up of men over sixty (they served for life) advised the Ephors and performed as judges. A large Assembly was open to all citizens over thirty, but its members' powers were very limited. They simply voted on matters previously discussed by the Ephors by shouting yes or no—the group that shouted loudest won!

The Plight of the Helots

We have already learned how the Spartans depended upon the labor of the Helots, an enslaved people who outnumbered them seven to one. The Helots were treated harshly; they were beaten if they did not produce sufficient crops, and they could even be put to death if they complained. All Helots had to be home by dusk, and no lights were allowed in their villages during the hours of darkness. Groups of young Spartan soldiers patrolled the streets at night with knives, killing any Helots who weren't in their houses. These miserable people must have hated their masters; they certainly had good reason to rebel (as they had in the sixth century), if only they could!

The need to keep the Helots in line explains why Sparta had the only full-time standing army in Greece. The city could proudly boast that it had no surrounding walls, because, as its leaders explained, "Sparta's ramparts are her men."

The Training of a Soldier

From the moment of birth, a Spartan's life was determined and molded by the army. A newborn baby was inspected by the Council of Elders; if they considered the child frail or abnormal in any way, it was abandoned on a hillside to die. The Spartans believed that only strong, healthy baby boys could become fine soldiers, just as only robust girls could become the mothers of future warriors. Clearly, soldiering was all that counted!

Spartan boys lived at home until they were seven, when they were sent off to military camp. There they were taught by older soldiers to obey orders without questioning them. The boys consumed a sparse amount of food, wore the skimpiest of clothing (they ran barefoot, even in the snow), and slept outside on piles of rushes in all kinds of weather. Every ten days they were lined up and examined to make sure they weren't getting fat! They exercised constantly, and they learned to fight and to endure hardship without complaining. Emotion was considered a sign of weakness, and a Spartan lad often bit his lip to stifle a cry of pain. Whipping contests were held at the camps to determine who could stand the most pain without crying; occasionally a boy would die rather than beg for an end to the lashes.

Sometimes the boys were given no food at all, so that they would learn to live off the land. They were even encouraged to steal, since a soldier's survival might depend upon his ability to obtain food in this way. A boy was punished if he was caught stealing, not because of the theft itself but because he had gotten caught! According to legend, a Spartan boy once hid a stolen fox under his tunic; when confronted by his teachers, he let the creature rip his chest open rather than admit to his theft. Another common camp activity was a stealing competition; the boys had to try to steal pieces of cheese while dodging blows from their teachers' whips!

A Soldier's Life

At the age of twenty a young man lived and trained in an army barracks. He was given a portion of land by the state and a number of Helots to work it and produce his food. (The Helots were allowed to keep a small amount of what they grew.) This left the Spartan free to pursue his military career. At the age of twenty-eight he was eligible to serve in the front line of the army.

Any man who married before the age of thirty had to visit his wife and children in secret! Yet, if he did not marry by the age of thirty-eight he was punished, and street gangs of women beat up uncommitted bachelors! But once married, a soldier continued to spend his time at the barracks; only old men actually lived with their wives in their own houses.

For the Spartans, then, the military life was the only life, and they focused all their energy into becoming invincible fighters. It was said that a Spartan soldier was worth at least ten of any other Greek hoplite. He was easily recognized by his long hair and his red cloak, and a steadily advancing line of red-cloaked fighters must have put fear into the hearts of any opposing army!

A Spartan was trained to fight to the death rather than retreat (remember the courageous stand of Leonidas at Thermopylae!). A Spartan mother once told her son to return from battle either with his shield or on it. The meaning of the message is clear: A coward would drop his heavy and cumbersome shield before deserting his post, while a heroic warrior would hold it until the moment of his death. After a battle, the bodies of slain soldiers were placed upon their shields and carried home by their comrades.

*fig. 74— **A Spartan soldier***

A Conservative Polis

The Spartans resisted change of any kind, because they feared that new ideas might weaken their strict regulations and thereby threaten their absolute control of the Helots. In fact, foreigners were not even allowed in Sparta! Spartan citizens were called *homoioi* which means "men who are similar"; there was no room for individuality in that harsh polis. And just as boys had to obey their teachers, soldiers displayed absolute obedience to command on the battlefield.

Sparta did have a small class of craftsmen called the *perioicoi* ("neighbors"); they were not full citizens, but they did serve in the army. They lived in small villages outside the city. Thanks to the work done by the Helots and the perioikoi, Sparta was able to remain self-sufficient. There was no trade with other city-states, and the currency used throughout the rest of Greece had no value in Sparta. Local products were simply exchanged (bartered), although sometimes iron bars were used to represent specific amounts.

Athens and Sparta, Two Dominant Powers

The Spartans had no time for reading and writing, since every moment had to be utilized for military procedures. Their simple life style became proverbial; our modern word "spartan" describes a situation marked by severe self-discipline. Music was encouraged, however, because it was useful for the soldiers to march to a rhythm.

And so while Athens experienced a flowering of art and drama, the Spartans remained close-minded and illiterate. These city-states, opposite in so many ways, remained the two major powers in Greece for a long time.

Questions:

1. Who were the Ephors?
2. Why did the Spartans believe that they needed to have a strong military state?
3. Describe the daily life of a Spartan teenage boy.
4. What does it mean to return home "either with your shield or on it"?
5. How was a Spartan soldier recognized?

Ideas to Think About:

1. Spartan girls were encouraged to participate in sports alongside the boys so that they would be strong, healthy mothers. In this respect, they had greater opportunities to interact with young men than did their counterparts in the other city-states. Not surprisingly, the Athenians belittled the Spartan women and considered them uncouth. In Sparta childbirth was considered the female equivalent of battle. In fact, the only Spartans honored in marked tombs were men killed in battle and women who died in childbirth!

2. A Spartan who didn't fight bravely was called a "trembler." He was forced to shave one side of his face and to keep a beard on the other. He was thus easily identifiable as the target of scorn and ridicule in his city.

3. Spartan food was often mocked by other Greeks. Most unappetizing of all was the famous Spartan black broth made from pork cooked in blood, vinegar and salt. An Athenian once

tasted this watery stew and then remarked that he finally understood why Spartans were so willing to die!

4. Sparta lies in the region of Laconia. As we have learned, the Spartans prided themselves on "roughing it," existing with few material comforts and wasting nothing. This philosophy also applied to the spoken word. Today, the word "laconic" means "expressing much in a few words" (concise). Here is an historic example of a laconic remark. When king Philip of Macedonia invaded Greece (more about him later), he hoped that the Spartans would not become involved in his battles against the other Greek city-states. If they did not stay put, he would have to invade their polis. Philip sent a messenger to Sparta to deliver a challenge that ended with the following words; "If we invade your city, we will raze it to the ground!" The Spartan reply was, quite simply, "If!"

5. The Spartans claimed that their unique way of life originated with a man named Lycurgus who lived around 850 B.C. He established the government of Kings and ephors. However, most scholars believe he was only a legendary hero.

Projects:

1. On poster board make a chart that compares and contrasts the systems of government in Athens and Sparta.

2. If you are a girl, would you prefer to have lived in Athens or Sparta? Give specific reasons for your choice.

3. The Spartans continued the ways of the Dorians. Write a paragraph describing how the Spartans perpetuated the life style of the warriors who conquered the Myceneans.

4. Can you think of a modern person or society that has a spartan lifestyle? Is it by choice or circumstances? Write a paragraph about the advantages of living with only the bare essentials.

Chapter XIV — DAILY LIFE IN ATHENS DURING THE GOLDEN AGE

A Greek House

The typical Athenian house stood beside a crooked, narrow street. It was constructed of sun-dried mud bricks laid over a framework of wooden beams on a stone base. The outer surface of the dwelling was covered with stucco (a plaster made of sand and crushed stone). The walls were so soft that burglars could easily cut through them; this explains why the Greek word for burglars (*toichorychoi*) literally means "wall diggers!" The inner walls of a larger home were decorated with fresco paintings. The pitched roof was covered with clay tiles. Near the main entrance of the house stood a statue of Hermes (called a Herm) whose main function was to ward off evil.

There were few windows facing the busy city street. Family life centered around an inner open-air courtyard where flowers bloomed in the bright sunshine. An altar was placed there for the offering of prayers to the gods. Slender columns surrounded the courtyard and supported a sloping roof; this encircling colonnade provided the family with shade in hot weather and shelter on rainy days. Facing on the courtyard were the kitchen, bathroom, and the men's dining area (the *andron*).

Bedrooms were usually on a second level, although more modest dwellings had only one floor. The woman of the house had separate quarters; a large room called the *gynaeceum*, where she could run the household, spin, weave, and entertain her friends. This is where the wife of an Athenian citizen spent most of her life. Her freedom was extremely limited, as we will see later in this chapter.

A Greek home had a sparse amount of furniture by modern standards—a few tables, chairs, beds and couches. But each piece was carefully carved and decorated by a skilled craftsman. The wealthy Athenians owned furnishings made of beautiful imported wood, such as red cedar from Lebanon and black ebony from Africa; these handsome pieces were often inlaid with gold, silver or ivory.

The *thronus* was a huge armchair used by the head of a well-to-do family (a very wealthy man might have one made of marble); in humbler residences the head of the family sat upon a simpler wooden armchair with a leather seat, his feet resting upon a footstool. A *klismos* was a straight-backed chair with no arms that was used by a guest of honor (and, at private family gatherings, by the woman of the house). Everyone else sat on plain stools that folded up for easy storage.

A bed and a dining couch (more about these later) were important pieces of furniture that had a similar design; each consisted of a wooden frame strung with leather thongs upon which was placed a mattress and pillows. Dining tables were often three-legged, and they were low so that they could be tucked under couches when they were not needed.

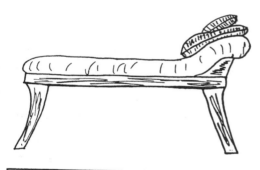

fig. 75 — **A dining couch**

The Greeks used wooden boxes of all sizes for the storage of spare clothing, blankets and armor, since there were no closets in their homes. Some everyday items, such as cups, baskets, and cloaks, were hung on metal hooks attached to the plaster walls. Room lighting was provided at night by a metal or pottery lamp containing olive oil and a wick (it must have been very dim!). Charcoal was burned in small portable metal braziers for heat during the winter months. Most of the smoke went out through a hole in the roof.

The household slaves obtained water for the family at a local spring, although a few wealthy citizens had private wells dug on their property. Clay pipes conducted dirty water from the bathrooms into an open drain that ran down the center of the street. Garbage was usually thrown into the street, where it was eaten by dogs and rodents. Small wonder that the living quarters of the house faced away from the smelly roadways and toward the pleasant inner courtyard!

How the Greeks Dressed

An Athenian man's everyday garment was a rectangular piece of wool woven by his wife. It was called a chiton. To get dressed, he simply wrapped the material loosely around his body and fastened it with a pin at one or both shoulders (depending on the latest fashion); the garment fell in folds to his lower thigh. It was gathered at the waist with a leather cord. Short sleeves could be fashioned by gathering and pinning some of the material at the upper arm. Long sleeves, however, were the sign of a slave or workman, and an Athenian citizen wouldn't dream of wearing them! The chiton was also the basic garment of Greek women, but theirs were ankle-length. Greek men generally wore light-colored or bleached white chitons (often decorated with a narrow border), while the women preferred material that was dyed and patterned with bright colors. Beginning in the fifth century B.C. some wealthy Greeks wore chitons made from cotton that was imported from India. Egyptian linen was another popular material for the summer months.

Greek men never wore trousers. Indeed, they considered them the mark of a barbarian! The standard footwear was the leather sandal, although most people went barefoot in the privacy of their homes.

fig. 76 — **A chiton**

A long cloak, called a *himation*, was often draped over one's chiton in cool weather. There was an art to draping a himation, and people who did not do it properly quickly became the object of ridicule! This is how it was done: One end of the cloak was placed at the waist under the right arm, the material was thrown over the left shoulder, pulled under the right arm, and then tossed over the left shoulder again. If the loose end was too long it would drag in the mud, and if it was too short, it would look silly. The Greeks must have practiced donning a himation for hours to get it right! A shorter cloak, called a *chlamlys*, was often worn by younger men.

The average Greek did not possess many articles of clothing, and so he had to take good care of what he had. Clothing thieves roamed the cities, and they were were quick to grab a chiton or himation while its owner was bathing or exercising. Sometimes a cloak was stolen right off its owners shoulders at night!

A chiton could be cleaned by a worker called a fuller. He made a paste from an aluminum salt (appropriately called "fuller's earth"). Then he rubbed the paste on the dirty cloth. When it dried the salt crumbled, and the fuller removed the residue (including the soiling) with a wire-toothed comb or brush. He then rinsed the cloth in clear water. To bleach a white chiton he hung it up in a room filled with sulphur fumes. Sometimes the fuller used human urine as a cleansing solution! Cleaning a chiton was an expensive process, and so the Greeks made great efforts to keep them unsoiled as long as possible.

Hair Styles and Cosmetics

In the days of Homer, Greek men wore their hair and beards long, but these were kept clipped and trimmed in the Golden Age. Not too short, however, because short-cropped hair was a sign of stinginess (a miserly man had his hair cut close to his head so that it would take longer to grow in, and thus he'd have to pay for fewer haircuts!). The Spartans, of course, always wore their hair long as a sign of strength (and also to cushion their hard metal helmets).

Most Greek women had long hair, although the wealthiest women wore wigs. During the Golden Age it was stylish to wear one's hair up, tied with ribbons, scarves, or pieces of golden jewelry. The hair of slave women, however, was usually clipped short.

A pale face was considered the most beautiful, and so powders made from white lead were often applied to a woman's skin to produce this effect. Of course, a pale complexion was also a sign of nobility, since it contrasted strikingly with the deeply tanned faces of the peasant and slave women who labored in the hot sun. A Greek lady held a mirror of polished bronze attached to a slender handle when she applied her make-up or simply wished to admire herself. She used alkanet root to redden her cheeks and soot to line her eyes; she anointed her body with sweet-smelling oils imported from Asia.

The Greeks loved jewelry, and the women wore many bracelets, necklaces, rings and drop earrings made of gold, silver, bronze, ivory, and bone. The jewelry of the wealthy was often adorned with precious stones such as lapis lazuli (a blue stone) and amber. Even the men enjoyed wearing metal rings, bracelets and headbands.

Morning

The average Athenian arose early, possibly awakened by the crowing of a rooster (a popular Persian import). He washed his face with the cool water in a pottery basin and cleaned his teeth by rubbing them with powdered pumice (volcanic ash).

Breakfast consisted of simple

fare—bread, cheese, fresh fruit such as pears, dates, or grapes, and perhaps a goblet of wine (which was always blended with water). Many Greeks were content to merely nibble on a lump of bread soaked in wine. After his morning meal a craftsman went to his workshop, probably a small room in the front of his house or one rented in another building; a more affluent citizen might spend a few hours studying the records of the crops produced on his estates. Morning was also the time when government business was attended to.

The Agora

Noon was market time, and the man of the house was responsible for the shopping (women were seldom seen on the street). The marketplace was called the *agora*; it was the heart of the city. Surrounded by columned porches (called *stoa*) and government buildings, the agora was a bustling place where merchants exhibited their wares in wooden booths and haggled over prices with their customers. Woven reed baskets displayed farm produce such as olives, lettuce, onions, cheese, poultry, eggs, and grain as well as freshly caught fish from the local ports. The meat and fish were often placed on marble slabs, because the cool stone kept them fresher longer. Small shops selling lamps, cooking pots, and luxury goods occupied some of the buildings lining the stoa.

The marketplace attracted foreign traders as well as local ones. Merchants from Asia displayed beautifully woven cloth and jewelry, while traders from Cyprus offered copper tools and containers. Employers also went to the agora to hire workmen or to purchase slaves.

An Athenian citizen could easily spend an entire afternoon at the agora, not merely shopping but also strolling among the colonnades and gossiping with his friends. Actually, the original meaning of the word "agora" was "meeting," since from earliest times people would gather in the town center to discuss common issues.

As we have learned, the Greeks were introduced to the concept of coinage by Lydian traders in the Archaic Age. At first, every polis issued its own coins, but after the Persian Wars Athenian money became the standard currency throughout Greece. The two major units were the obol and the drachma (one drachma equalled six obols). The average Athenian citizen earned about one half a drachma (three obols) per day. No one in Greece carried a purse, and chitons had no pockets, so a merchant often put his coins in his cheek for safekeeping!

A Visit to the Gymnasium

Apollo embodied the Greek ideal of a strong and healthy body as well as a well educated mind. The word *arete* means "excellence in everything", and it was the goal of every Greek citizen. An important part of an Athenian's day was, therefore, a visit to the gymnasium, the ancient equivalent of a modern sports center, where he could work out to keep his body in prime condition.

The gymnasium was a large building with plenty of space to run, throw a discus or practice many of the other events performed in the Olympic Games. First, however, a man removed his clothing and handed it to his slave, who guarded it while his master was working out (remember those "chiton snatchers!"). The word "gymnasium" comes from the Greek *gymnos* which means "naked," for Greek athletes did not want their actions to be hindered by their loose-fitting garments. After undressing, the man entered the anointing room, where he covered his body with olive oil and then scraped it clean with a metal instrument called a strigil. This procedure removed dirt and sweat, and it was repeated after exercising.

A strenuous physical workout in the gymnasium was often followed by a refreshing bath. Afterwards, the man could put on his chiton and stroll back to the agora to converse with his friends and neighbors in the cool shade of the stoa. What a pleasant way to spend the day!

The Evening Meal

An Athenian family enjoyed a cooked meal in the late evening after the heat of the sun had dissipated and refreshing breezes cooled the house. The man of the household reclined on a couch, propping himself up with his left arm on soft pillows and eating with his right hand. His wife served him and the children, and then she sat down on her straight-backed chair. Sometimes the family was served by their slaves.

fig. 77 — **Man reclining on a dining couch**

Dinner was the main meal of the day, and it consisted of bread, fruit (figs and dates), nuts, vegetables (peas, lettuce, cabbage or lentils), cheese, and perhaps salted fish. The Greeks normally ate red meat only after animals were sacrificed at religious ceremonies. Cheese was made from goats' milk (cows' milk was considered fit only for calves!). Onions and garlic garnished the fish and vegetables, and coriander and sesame were popular seasonings. Cakes saturated with honey made a delicious dessert. The wine was diluted with water in large jugs called kraters. It was then poured into wide pottery goblets with two handles. Of course, the children drank goat's milk.

Banquets and Symposia

Frequently a man of comfortable means invited a few friends to his home for an all-male banquet. The number of guests would always range between three and nine (no less than the three Graces and no more than the nine Muses of mythology). The banquet took place in the men's quarters of the home (the andron). The host's wife directed the preparation and serving of the meal; then she was obliged to remain in the gynaeceum until the banquet was over and it was time to clean up!

While family meals were fairly simple affairs, a banquet was often elaborate. Upon their arrival, the guests removed their sandals so that the household slaves could wash their feet. Then they took their places on the couches.

The main course of a banquet was usually fresh fish—some favorite dishes were fried shrimp, baked turbot with mulberry sauce, and bass steamed in brine with vegetables. Fowl such as thrush baked in honey or duck roasted with raisins were a special treat. The next course was nuts, fruit and cheese, followed by sweet cakes.

The food was served on pottery or metal plates which were placed upon low tables beside the dining couches. The men ate with their fingers. Metal spoons were sometimes used for liquid dishes, but usually a piece of bread made an efficient scoop (forks would not be invented for a thousand years.) A diner wiped his greasy hands on a piece of bread, which he then threw to the dogs!

Wine flowed abundantly at the banquets, although we must remember that it was diluted (its alcoholic content was considerably less than that of modern beer). Lime, resin or seawater were frequently added to the wine to cut down on its acidity. Even today Greek wine often contains resin (this wine is called *retsina*). It was a time-honored tradition to spill a little wine on the floor at the beginning of a meal as an offering to the gods; this was an early form of saying grace.

After the meal, the men discussed all sorts of topics, from local politics to the pettiest gossip. Of course, the wine continued to be poured, and so this part of the evening's entertainment was called the *symposium*, which means "drinking together". Sometimes symposia were held without a preceding banquet. (Today a symposium is a meeting of scholarly people to discuss particular subjects.)

During a Greek symposium the guests anointed their hair and beards with myrrh, and they placed wreaths upon their heads and around their necks. A toss of the dice selected a toastmaster for the evening who proposed toasts and selected topics for discussion; he also set the proportions of water to wine (perhaps the amount of wine increased as the evening wore on!). Occasionally the men were entertained by musicians and dancing girls.

A symposium could become a rowdy affair, since the Greeks did not frown upon becoming drunk. In fact, intoxication was considered a sign of wealth, since working men could not afford to deal with a hangover the next morning! The merry-making might last until the early hours of the morning, and the wife and slaves of the household would be busy all the next day putting everything back in order!

The people of the lower classes had neither the time nor the money to engage in such activities as banquets and symposia. In the evenings they had a hearty meal of barley porridge sweetened with honey (or perhaps thick pea soup), cheese, onions, figs, and wine.

The Role of Greek Women

The life of a typical Greek woman was far less interesting than that of her husband, for she lived in a man's world. Most of her time was spent in the gynaeceum of her home (don't confuse gynaeceum with gymnasium!). She hardly ever ventured out of her home, and then only when she was accompanied by another woman or a slave. If she attended the theater, she had to sit in the back row with the foreigners, and she could only see a tragedy since comedy was considered too bawdy for her delicate ears.

The duties of the wife of an Athenian citizen were simply to run the household, to spin wool and weave cloth for the family's clothing and blankets, and to raise the children. Greek women had no say in the government. They were not even allowed to own property or to conduct legal transactions. And so, from birth to death a woman was under the control of some male relative, be it her father, her husband, or her son. If she had no husband or son, her life was in the hands of her brother or her nearest male relative.

A man could divorce his wife simply by making a statement of his intentions in front of witnesses. A woman, however, could do no such thing, since she had no legal rights. In the case of a divorce, the husband kept the children and sent his former wife back to her family! He had to return her dowry, though.

Pericles once said that the ideal woman was the one who attracted the least attention. Even the great philosopher Aristotle defined woman as an imperfect form of man! For all their wisdom, the ancient Greeks had much to learn about equal rights!

It is important to remember, however, that Spartan women had much more freedom than their counterparts in the other city-states. They were encouraged to interact with the men, they competed in athletic events, and they could travel where ever they pleased.

An Athenian marriage was arranged by the fathers of the bride and groom. By the age of thirty a man was well established in business and able to afford a comfortable life style for his bride; he usually wed a young woman half his age so that she could serve him for many years. The family of the bride paid the groom a dowry (a gift of property or money).

Before her wedding, a girl placed her dolls upon the altar at a temple of Artemis. This act symbolized her coming of age—her putting aside of all childish ways. The bride wore bright clothing and a veil to her wedding. At the start of the ceremony an animal was sacrificed, and then its gall bladder was removed "lest bitterness mar the marriage." Often a bride saw her husband for the first time at the altar of marriage! After the solemn vows were taken, the guests threw grain and fruit at the couple, just as we throw rice today. This was their way of asking the gods to grant the couple many children. Afterwards, the husband carried his bride over the threshold of their new house, and they ate a special cake together.

Early Childhood

When a baby was born in Athens, the father had the right to accept or reject it. As in Sparta, a weak or frail child was rejected by the father and left on a lonely hillside to die from exposure (the lucky ones were adopted by families, for whom they became slaves). All too frequently in that male-dominated society, a baby was rejected simply because it was a girl.

A boy was usually named for his paternal grandfather. Greek names had special meanings. For example, Pericles means "very famous," Alcibiades means "son of a strong one," and Aristocles means "the best".

Athenian children up to the age of seven were raised by their mother and her slaves in the family home. If a child misbehaved, he might be threatened with a visit from Mormo (a monster who ate children) or Empusa (a hobgoblin who changed into many frightening shapes)! In general, though, the lives of Greek children were care-free; they were greatly doted upon by their parents as they played happily in the warm Mediterranean sunlight.

Education

When Cleisthenes was in power he ordered all citizens to educate their sons (the girls stayed at home to learn domestic tasks). A special slave called a *pedagogue* taught his young master manners and escorted him to school (today "pedagogue" means "teacher"). At school the boy was taught to read, write, and to do math using an abacus. He held a metal stylus (pen) to practice writing upon a waxed tablet, and any mistakes he made were easily rubbed out. When the coating of wax became thin, a new layer was melted over it and the tablet was as good as new. Older boys wrote upon papyrus (a kind of paper made by the Egyptians) using pen and ink.

The young students studied the great myths and legends of the past, and they often memorized hundreds of lines from Homer or Hesiod. They also learned to dance, sing, and play the flute or lyre. Indeed, a well-educated Athenian gentleman was expected to be able to play the lyre and sing whenever called upon; "he who doesn't know how to play the lyre" was a proverbial description of an uneducated person! Of course, instruction in athletic events was an important part of a schoolboy's education, and he worked out at the gymnasium every day.

A boy completed his education at the age of fifteen. Then he could become an apprentice to a craftsman or learn about his father's business.

At the age of eighteen a young man was eligible to become a citizen. A special ceremony was held in his honor at the temple of Zeus, where he was given the shield and spear of a warrior; he then swore an oath of citizenship, promising to be a good soldier, to preserve the Athenian constitution and to respect the Greek religion. A lock of his hair was cut and dedicated to the god of the heavens. Following the ceremony, a banquet was given in honor of the new citizen by his male relatives.

Military Obligations

Upon becoming a citizen, an Athenian began his two years of military training. When he was twenty he signed up for active duty; he would be called up if Athens went to war. Soldiers were obliged to supply their own equipment, and the richer the man, the better his armor and weapons. A wealthy man had a bronze (or iron) helmet, breastplate, and greaves as well as metal strips to protect his thighs. He might even ride a horse. A poor man had no armor except his shield. For obvious reasons, many of the poorest men chose to become rowers in the Athenian fleet!

Slaves in Athens

Slaves have been frequently mentioned in this chapter. It is probably surprising for you to learn that in the city acknowledged to be the birthplace of democracy nearly every family had slaves! The average household had three, but a wealthy man might have fifty. Even a family of modest means probably had at least one slave to do menial tasks. In 431 B.C. slaves made up about one third of the population of Attica.

Who were the slaves? They were usually the captives of war (or the children of captives), although some were purchased in the slave markets. Fortunately, the lives of the Greek slaves were not terribly hard. Those who were skilled often worked side by side with free Greek artisans and merchants. Many slaves were paid a small amount for their labors, and this made it possible for some of them to eventually buy back their freedom. However, those slaves who were condemned to work in the silver mines of Attica led truly wretched lives. They were branded and chained together, and they often died of exhaustion.

Athenian democracy actually depended upon slavery. Were it not for the labor provided by the slaves, the Athenian citizens would not have been able to attend government meetings, serve on juries, or discuss political matters in the agora. This is one of history's great ironies.

The Metics

Metics were foreign-born (non-Athenian) merchants, tradesmen and artists who made up a significant part of the middle class in Athens. There were about half as many metics as there were slaves. The metics were taxed, and they were expected to serve in the army; however, they could not own land, marry into a family of citizens, or vote. The metics, along with the slaves and the freedmen (former slaves), were the backbone of the Athenian economy.

Questions:

1. Describe the basic layout of an Athenian house.
2. What was a gynaeceum?
3. How were the houses lighted at night?
4. What was a himation and how was it worn?
5. Describe the agora.
6. What were the major units of Athenian money?
7. What took place at the gymnasium?
8. What was the role of a typical Athenian woman?
9. What was a symposium?
10. Describe the education of the son of a Greek citizen.

Ideas to Think About:

1. When a boy was born in Athens, an olive wreath was hung on the door of his house to announce the good news to the neighbors. The birth of a girl was a less joyful occasion, for which a plain wooden circle or tuft of wool was placed on the door. Thus, from the very beginning of their lives females were treated as inferior human beings.

2. In Athens there were special officials to check weights and measures. They were called the *metronomoi*; ten men were chosen for the position each year. Another group of officials, the *agoranomoi*, checked the quality of products being sold in the agora. A third group was the money changers; they were called *trapezitai* "tablemen" because they worked at tables in the marketplace. They exchanged one kind of coins for another, charging a fee for each transaction, and they made so much profit that eventually they began to lend money out. This was the beginning of banking.

3. The Greeks loved horses. Ownership of one of those splendid beasts was the sign of an aristocrat. In fact, the Greek word horse (*hippos*) is included in many aristocratic names: the father of Pericles was named Xanthippos (meaning "tawny horse"), and the father of Alexander the Great (more about him later) was Philhippos ("horse lover"). When a Greek aristocrat died, his horse was always present at his funeral.

4. A son inherited his father's property, and if there was more than one, they would share it equally. If there was no son, a daughter could inherit, but she was required to marry the man chosen by her father, and he (the husband) became the actual heir.

5. Childbirth was a dangerous experience. There was no anaesthesia to reduce pain and no medicine to prevent infection. Women were expected to have as many children as possible, since so many died at birth. Those women who survived the average of ten childbirths seldom lived beyond thirty-five or forty. Men on the other hand, could expect to live ten years longer than women.

Projects:

1. The Greeks decorated their clothing and pottery with geometric designs, and many of these are copied by modern artists. In fact, the swastika, the insignia of Nazi Germany, is a Greek design found on many ancient vases. Find other examples of Greek designs that are used today and draw them on a poster.

2. Make your own chiton. Take a large (king-sized) pillowcase. Cut a hole at one end for your head to slip through and two smaller holes near the top on the two sides for your arms. Decorate the bottom border of the garment with Greek geometric designs. Use a piece of cloth tied at the waist as a sash. A longer, roomier chiton can be fashioned from an old sheet following the same pattern. Wear the chiton for the performance of a Greek play or for a Greek party.

3. See if you can properly drape a himation. Cut up an old sheet or blanket (get permission first!) into two pieces, and then sew them together to make one long piece of material. Using the directions on page 145, drape yourself with the cloak. Better still, wear it over the chiton you've already made (project # 2 above).

4. Have a Greek banquet. Everyone in the class can bring in a dish of typical Greek food (such as stuffed grape leaves, cucumbers in yogurt, or baklava). The specialties have not changed much over the centuries! Wear chitons (see #2 above) and bring pillows to recline upon while dining. Be sure to have a lot of finger food, because forks are not allowed!

PART III — THE LATER YEARS

Chapter XV — THE PELOPONNESIAN WAR

Resentment Of Athens Builds

Despite the phenomenal achievements of Athens during the Golden Age (or perhaps because of them), the members of the Delian League continued to grumble among themselves. They cherished their long tradition of independence, and the concept of a unified Greece seemed unnatural. Furthermore, the Athenians, who prided themselves on protecting the rights of individual citizens, were viewed by many of their Greek kinsmen as authoritarian tyrants.

There were economic problems as well. Corinth, for example, had long enjoyed its status as a wealthy commercial center. But since the defeat of the Persians, the focal point of trade had shifted from Corinth to the Athenian port of Pireaus. The Corinthians wished that Athens had never existed!

Sparta Is Drawn Into the Conflict

The Spartans had never joined the Delian league. They depended upon their highly renowned military prowess to hold off any enemy attack, and since their city was located well inland, they had few worries about the Persian fleet. However, they did become increasingly concerned about Athens' expanding sphere of influence. We must remember that Sparta was run by military leaders who wished to maintain the status-quo at all costs. The idea of change made them cringe! So they worried about their territories being surrounded by democratic city-states controlled by Athens. Where would it all lead?

Sparta's displeasure was well-known throughout southern Greece, and when certain city-states of the Peloponnese decided they could no longer tolerate the over-bearing Athenians, they naturally looked to the red-cloaked warriors for support. Eventually a series of minor skirmishes drew the Spartans into the conflict. The Spartan Alliance united the city-states of the Peloponnese, Corinth, and the region of Boeotia under the leadership of Sparta.

War Breaks Out

Mainland Greece was now divided into two confederations: the Delian

League and the Spartan Alliance. It took only a minor incident involving a trading dispute to start the sparks flying, and in 431 B.C. war broke out. Called the Peloponnesian War by the Athenians, this unfortunate struggle of Greek versus Greek would last thirty years.

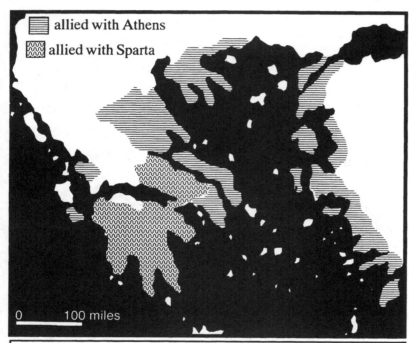

allied with Athens

allied with Sparta

0   100 miles

fig. 78 — **The two confederations**

Thucydides Chronicles the War

Fortunately for us, the major events of the war were carefully recorded and documented by a Greek historian named Thucydides in his book THE PELOPONNESIAN WAR. Thucydides actually fought in the war (on the Athenian side) and took copious notes after each battle. He spoke with many of the military leaders in order to more fully understand their strategies, and he described these conversations in great detail in his book. He also interviewed eyewitnesses to the fighting and carefully examined the battlesites. Unlike Herodotus, Thucydides did not exaggerate figures or offer his personal views about events; rather, he maintained a methodical and objective approach in describing historical events. Thus, although Herodotus is considered the Father of History, Thucydides was the first to impartially report on the major occurrences of his time.

A Ten-Year Stalemate

Pericles was in power in Athens when the war began. He recognized the superiority of the Spartan soldiers, and so he did all he could to avoid land battles, relying instead upon Athens' naval power. He was reassured by the two towering stone walls connecting the city with the seaport Piraeus (see p. 121), for he knew that as long as the Athenian fleet ruled the seas, he could depend upon a steady supply of food from abroad. He hoped that eventually the Spartans would run out of supplies and leave Athens alone.

For ten long years the war continued with neither side winning an advantage. Every summer, the Spartans ravaged the fields of Attica, destroying the grain, vineyards and olive groves with the aim of breaking the will of the Athenian people. During these trying times, the farmers and landowners sought refuge within the walls of the city. Meanwhile, the Athenian ships raided the coast of the Peloponnese, destroying whatever enemy ships they encountered. And so the war dragged on, no one able to break the impasse.

Pericles Inspires the Athenians

Pericles knew that he needed to encourage his people to endure the hardships caused by the war. He seized the occasion of a battle in which many Athenian soldiers had been slain to give a moving speech. After briefly praising the fallen soldiers, he proudly boasted of the great city for which they had given their lives. He described Athens as a shining light whose way of life would one day be copied by cities around the Greek world. (His entire speech appears in the Appendix, p. 211) As he had hoped, his words gave the Athenians the will to persevere in their struggle.

The Plague

The frequent sieges of the rather crowded city created uncomfortable and unsanitary living conditions, and the daily lives of the Athenians steadily deteriorated until a crisis arose. In 430 B.C., ships bearing grain from Egypt arrived at the port of Piraeus. Unfortunately, along with their cargo they carried infected rats which raced along the walled corridor to Athens. Fleas from the rodents bit and infected the Athenians, causing a terrible plague to break out. Ironically, the high stone walls confined the deadly disease to the city and spared the enemy soldiers stationed outside. Athens' lifeline had become an avenue of death!

One quarter of the population died, including Pericles himself. The passing of that highly respected leader marked a turning point in the Athenians' resistance to the Spartan advances. Matters grew steadily worse when Pericles was succeeded by men who lacked his judgment and authority.

The Role of the Persians

The Persians played an important part in the Peloponnesian War. They well remembered their humiliating defeats at Salamis and Platea and the ensuing loss of the Ionian colonies. Over the years since then, Persian kings had sided with Sparta against the rapidly growing Delian League. During the Peloponnesian War the Persians supplied the Spartan Alliance with the resources to build up an impressive fleet of ships. They undoubtedly relished the thought of the Greek city-states going at each other, a process that would inevitably weaken them all. Furthermore, they hoped that an Athenian defeat would restore to them their long lost territory in Ionia.

At the same time, the Persians understood the ways of the iron-handed Spartans whose government strongly resembled their own absolute monarchy. They were puzzled by the Athenian system that placed power in the hands of the ordinary people.

A Fatal Mistake

In spite of the aid the Persians gave to the Spartans, the war continued to drag on. In 421 B.C. both sides acknowledged their weariness with the whole thing and agreed to a temporary peace. The Greek people slowly returned to a more normal way of life, and all was well. But eight years later the peace was broken when the Athenians made an unwise decision: They attacked the city of Syracuse on the island of Sicily in order to obtain a new source of grain and cattle. They hoped that the conquest of Syracuse would make them the masters of the trade routes in the western Mediterranean.

The invasion was planned by a kinsman of Pericles named Alcibiades. He was a vain, selfish and impudent man who had gained power in the Athenian government through his guile and charm. The campaign was a military disaster from the beginning, and many Greek lives were lost. Those soldiers who survived the battles became the slaves of the Sicilians; they were condemned to labor in stone quarries for the rest of their lives. The Greek fleet was partially destroyed, and although new ships were later built, the Athenian navy never recovered its former strength. Athens had lost her mastery of the seas, and Sparta gained an overwhelming advantage.

The End of the War

In 405 B.C. the Spartan navy, led by Lysander, surprised the Athenian fleet off the coast of Ionia and destroyed all its ships while the crews were inland enjoying a good meal! The victorious Spartans now controlled the seas as well as the land. This was a fatal blow for Athens, because it severed the city's lifeline to the grain, timber and iron in the Greek colonies surrounding the Black Sea. When the Spartan ships blockaded Piraeus, the Athenians had no choice but to surrender.

Under the terms of the peace treaty, Athens gave up any surviving vessels and agreed to the destruction of all fortifications. The Athenian people watched in sorrow as the great walls that surrounded their city and extended to Piraeus were torn down by slaves working to the music of flutes. The Spartans rewarded the Persians for their support during the war by giving them the Ionian cities.

Although they were urged by some of their allies to kill the men of Athens, the Spartans refused to do so; they still remembered the heroism of the Athenian soldiers at the Battle of Marathon.

Sparta's Rule Is Short-lived

Sparta established a Council of Governors to rule Athens. A group of anti-democratic autocrats known as the Thirty Tyrants made life miserable for nearly everyone until they were finally deposed after a year in 403 B.C. The democratic government was restored, and Athens became a center of learning.

Yet, the brilliant flame of optimism and creativity that was ignited by the Greek success in the Persian Wars was nearly snuffed out by the Athenian defeat in the Peloponnesian debacle. Scholars living in the aftermath of that war began to question whether it was possible to achieve happiness in an often hostile world.

The Theban Phalanx

Sparta did not maintain military control over the rest of Greece indefinitely. In the fourth century B.C. a brilliant Theban general named Epaminondas devised a way to defeat the formidable Spartan soldiers. He knew that in a classic phalanx battle the winners were those soldiers who could push the hardest and break through the opposing line. Therefore, he restructured his formation so that the front line moved at an oblique angle, the left side considerably ahead of the right. He then strengthened the left flank by increasing the ranks from eight to fifty of his best fighting men. So, by the time the Theban center faced that of the enemy phalanx, its left flank had already broken through the right side of the enemy line. With the enemy's right flank thrown into disarray, the protruding Theban left flank could move inward to support the soldiers in the center. By the time the Theban soldiers on the right flank encountered the opposing phalanx, they were joined by the soldiers from the left and center sections. Now, the entire army crashed through what remained of the enemy line like a giant battering ram!

time, the Thebans, with numbers far less than those of the Spartan troops, trounced the legendary red-cloaked warriors; at the Battle of Leuctra (371 B.C.) they proved themselves to be the best soldiers in Greece. After their victory, they freed the Helots of Messenia. Sparta never recovered.

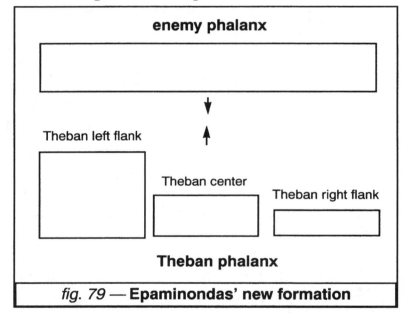

fig. 79 — **Epaminondas' new formation**

It was a simple strategy. The rapidly shifting front lines allowed the Theban soldiers to deliver a series of punches that were difficult for any army to withstand. The Spartans, trained for generations to march together in a straight line, were unprepared for such a change in tactics. Nor were they inclined to revise the traditional formation that had served them so well for so long. Within a short period of

Questions:

1. Why did many city-states resent Athens?
2. Why didn't the Spartans join the Delian League?
3. Who were the members of the Spartan Alliance?
4. What was Pericles' strategy?
5. How did the plague come to Athens?
6. What was the role of the Persians in the war?
7. What was Athens' fatal mistake?
8. What were the peace terms?
9. Describe Epaminondas' revolutionary battle plan.
10. Why was Thebes able to defeat Sparta?

Ideas to Think About

1. The funeral oration given by Pericles during the Peloponnesian War has frequently been compared with Lincoln's Famous Gettysburg Address (see Appendix p. 211). Both leaders spoke of the heroism of the soldiers who had given their lives for their homeland and of the need for those still alive to carry on the battle. It is for the living, they said, to make sure that the ideals the soldiers have died for will not perish. Both speeches were delivered at a time when a people was feeling discouraged about a long drawn-out war. They sought to inspire the people to continue the struggle. Despite the fact that they were written many many years apart, they are amazingly similar in content and outlook.

2. Pindar was a poet living in Thebes who was famous for beautiful odes about the Olympic Games. He disapproved of Athens' determination to make every city-state a democracy, and he accurately predicted that the self-righteousness of the Athenians would bring about their own ruin.

3. Although he was a gifted military strategist, Alcibiades was perhaps the worst scoundrel in Greek history. He was a self-centered opportunist, com-pletely lacking in scruples! Before leaving Athens to fight in Syracuse, he and some friends apparently went on a drunken rampage and defaced a group of stone statues of Hermes. When he was later summoned home to answer to the charges, he fled to Sparta. Once there, he told the Spartans how to attack an important town in Attica, and then he seduced the wife of one of the kings. For this he was condemned to death. Now he was a public enemy in both Athens and Sparta! But he used his charm to convince the Athenians to let him return, promising to get the Persians to help them against Sparta. He did manage to gain some Persian support (the Persians were always happy to play off one Greek city against another), and he later led an army against Sparta. Eventually his history of deceit caught up with him, and he found himself exiled once again from Athens. This time he sought refuge in Persia where, according to some accounts, he was later assassinated.

4. After the Peloponnesian War, many Greek soldiers became mercenaries (professional fighters for hire to other nations). A group of ten thousand Greek soldiers went to Babylonia (in modern Iraq) to fight for the Persian

Prince, Cyrus. He was killed and they found themselves abandoned far from home, the targets of the troops of Cyrus' brother. The Persians killed the Greek leaders, and the soldiers marched northwest for 600 miles, fighting off enemy attacks, crossing mountains, and surviving extremely harsh weather conditions. They finally made it to the Black Sea, where they marched from city to city along the coast (these were Greek cities) until they finally reached their homeland. Known as the Ten Thousand, they became heroes of the Greeks. The march was described by the Greek historian Xenophon, who had participated in it.

5. Thucydides was intrigued by the contrasting cultures of Sparta and Athens. Here is a statement he made about them in his book: "If the city of the (Spartans) had been abandoned, and the temples and the foundations of the buildings remained, great, I think, would be the disbelief of its power over such a long time from the past to the fame of the Spartans today. Athens, suffering from the same thing, would seem to have had twice the power than it does, judging from the appearance of the city"

(translation by Daniel Arnaud)

Projects:

1. Find out more about Athens' ill-fated attack upon Syracuse. Present a report about the battle to the class. Draw a map showing the location of Syracuse.

2. Carefully study Pericles' funeral oration and Abraham Lincoln's Gettysburg Address in the Appendix. Then write a short report comparing and contrasting the two speeches. Be sure to describe the historical circumstances in which they were presented.

3. "Lysistrata" is a play by Aristophanes in which the women of Athens find a clever and practical solution to the Peloponnesian War. Find out what the solution was. Then write your own (short) version of the play, and present it with several classmates.

4. Write a short play about the adventures and exploits of Alcibiades. Present it to the class.

5. "Persia was the real winner of the Peloponnesian War." What is the meaning of this statement? Do you agree or not? Write a short paper justifying your opinion.

Chapter XVI — THE GREAT PHILOSOPHERS

Lovers of Wisdom

By the fifth century B.C. most serious thinkers in Athens had discarded the mythological explanations of natural phenomena and looked for more logical answers to their questions about the universe. We will learn more about the early scientists in a later chapter.

The scholars who lived in Athens after the Peloponnesian War were particularly concerned about man's place in nature. *Philosopher* is a Greek word that means "lover of wisdom." In ancient Greece all scholars were considered philosophers. Today, however, philosophy has a stricter meaning: it is the study of human conduct and the principles by which the members of a society can live together in harmony.

In this chapter we will learn about three Greek scholars who were philosophers in the modern sense of the word. Socrates, Plato and Aristotle were brilliant men representing three generations of Athenians. They were intrigued by questions about morality and ethics (the rules and values of a civilized society). They pondered the meaning of happiness, and they wondered how it could be attained.

Socrates Asks Questions

Socrates lived from 470 until 399 B.C. As a young man he had fought in the Peloponnesian War; he once saved the life of Alcibiades. Afterwards he served in the Ecclesia. Socrates was greatly concerned about the effect the defeat by the Spartans had upon the spirit of the Athenian citizens. A huge number of young soldiers had been killed in that long, drawn-out war, commerce was at a standstill, and the vineyards and olive groves of Attica had been virtually destroyed. It was a very difficult time for everyone. Even after the Thirty Tyrants were booted out of power and a democratic government was restored, the new Athenian leaders lacked the confidence and optimism of Pericles. Athens was no longer the ruler of a great empire, and its leaders were groping for a new definition of their polis. They were uncertain and insecure, and because of this they nervously resisted any criticism of their policies. It seemed as though nearly everyone living in Athens was unhappy.

Socrates wondered about this malaise, and he tried to figure out how the Athenians could recapture the old joie de vivre (love of life) of the Golden Age. He decided that the people were simply confused and overwhelmed by the destructiveness of recent events. Perhaps by turning away from the troubling past and looking deep within their own souls, they could create a more positive attitude. Socrates was convinced that knowledge of the world began with the understanding of one's self, and he fervently proclaimed, "the unexamined life is not worth living."

He wandered about the agora, asking questions of everyone. "What is justice? What is wisdom? How do you define truth?" His most disconcerting question was, "Do you really understand what you're talking about?" Before long he had quite a large following of intellectual young citizens who were intrigued with his refusal to accept anything at face value. Socrates inquired of nearly anyone he met how men should behave, why something was good or beautiful when something else was not, and how a polis should best be governed. Whenever a question was answered, he immediately asked another. An encounter with Socrates must have been an exhausting experience! His systematic approach to learning was to start with a general topic and to slowly narrow it down to its essential parts until he got to the heart of the matter. By stripping away preconceived notions and unnecessary data like the peels of a banana, a person could arrive at the truth. This procedure is called deductive reasoning.

Socrates believed that the gods had created the world for mankind, and therefore men should be god-fearing. But when he spoke of the gods, he referred to them as a single, all-powerful force. Thus he spoke of God rather than the gods, and this blasphemy (attack on the established religion) helped to bring about his ruin.

fig. 80 — **Socrates**

The Athenian Government Is Vexed

The Athenian leaders felt extremely uncomfortable about Socrates' relentless questioning. Times had certainly changed. Pericles would have welcomed such a lively spirit of inquiry, but the officials of this era felt threatened by it. Furthermore, by emphasizing personal values Socrates seemed to suggest that the individual was more important than the state. Such an idea went counter to the traditions of Athens. And so when Socrates refused to stop his interminable questioning he was arrested. The government accused him of corrupting the young people by making them reconsider the role of the gods, and they called him a heretic (someone who opposes the official religion).

Trial and Conviction

Socrates had an opportunity to escape from his prison cell, but he refused to do so because he did not believe in breaking the law. At his trial he called himself "a gadfly" of the Athenian government; just as a fly bites a tired old horse and makes it jump, he questioned government policies in order to wake up the Athenians to the need for reform. He insisted that he was performing a helpful and necessary function for which they, his accusers, should be thankful!

Socrates probably could have saved himself, but he refused to admit to any wrong-doing. What was wrong with asking questions? The jury found him arrogant and terribly unsettling, and

they sentenced him to death. He was seventy years old.

In those days a guilty citizen was forced to drink a poisonous brew made from hemlock (the lower classes met more unpleasant ends). Socrates was surrounded by his weeping friends and followers when the brew was brought to him. Before he drank it, he chivalrously thanked the jailer who handed it to him, remarking that now he would have the good fortune to find out what death was like. He was curious to the end!

Enter Plato

Socrates never wrote anything down, but fortunately one of his pupils kept a detailed record of his words. This pupil was nick-named Plato, an epithet meaning "broad-shouldered" (his real name was Aristocles), and he lived from 427 until 347 B.C. Soon after the death of Socrates, Plato wrote an account of the trial and last moments of his master; entitled THE APOLOGY, it glorifies the life and teachings of Socrates.

Plato's Ideal State

Plato also wrote a series of essays called THE DIALOGUES. They resemble the script of play in which people discuss issues of government and everyday living. Of course, they are based upon the conversations Socrates had with his followers in the agora. Plato's longest dialogue, THE REPUBLIC, describes his vision of the ideal government. He did not support the democratic beliefs of Pericles (indeed, he felt that large groups of people often made bad decisions). Rather, he believed that society should be governed by an educated elite of philosophers. Included in this group were women, a notion not entertained by any of the other great thinkers of Greece. He was certainly ahead of his time!

Plato had a theory that all visible, tangible objects are unreal and that the things that we see are merely copies of ideas (which are real). Today such abstract reasoning about ideas and reality is contained in a science known as metaphysics.

A poet and a scholar, Plato later opened a school for intellectual young citizens in an olive grove near Athens. Because this land was dedicated to the legendary hero, Academeus, the school was called the Academy. Teachers and students gathered there to discuss the intricacies of math, science and philosophy. Plato taught there for nearly fifty years. Today, an academy is a place of learning.

Aristotle's Thirst For Knowledge

The third of the great Greek philosophers was Aristotle (384-322 B.C.), a pupil of Plato. Aristotle also questioned the meaning of such concepts as truth and beauty, but his greatest interest was the natural world. He carefully examined the biological structure of living things, and he arranged all the plants and animals he knew about into categories. He believed that everything had a special place in the universe.

Aristotle was also intrigued with human political structures, and in THE POLITICS he wrote that men should use their logic rather than their emotions to govern themselves (remember Euripides?). He agreed with Plato that people of education and talent should rule the polis. He justified slavery by arguing that non-Greeks were inferior beings who ought to serve their betters, the Greeks. His interest in literature is reflected in THE POETICS, a masterful work that includes a thoughtful and comprehensive analysis of drama and how it reflects Greek society.

Like his mentor Plato, Aristotle set up his own school in Athens. Called the Lyceum, it was a pleasant place where the teachers walked around the *peripatoi* (a columned porch in the garden), sharing their knowledge and wisdom with their students much as Socrates had once done. For this reason, Aristotle and his followers were known as the "peripatetics." Today a peripatetic is a person who is always on the move.

Aristotle was the first Greek scientist to follow a systematic method of inquiry and observation, and he wrote many books about his discoveries. He became so famous that King Philip of Macedonia asked him to teach his thirteen-year-old son, Alexander. We shall learn more of this relationship in the next chapter.

Questions:

1. What does the word "philosopher" mean?
2. Why were the Athenians unhappy?
3. What was the most important thing in life, according to Socrates?
4. Why was Socrates condemned by the government officials?
5. What was the Academy?
6. How did Plato feel about the democratic ideas of Pericles?
7. Who made the best governors, according to Plato?
8. What was Aristotle's greatest interest?
9. What does the word "peripatetic" mean?
10. Who was Aristotle's most famous pupil?

Ideas to Think About

1. Today teachers often use the Socratic method in the classroom. Like Socrates, they encourage students to ask questions about what they are learning rather than to simply accept what is written in a book. Do you find that group discussions (with thought-provoking questions tossed about) help you to understand what you are studying?

2. A student of Socrates once visited the Oracle of Delphi. The oracle proclaimed that the philosopher was wise, and at his trial Socrates referred to this description of himself. He then added that he must be the wisest of all men since he alone knew that he knew nothing!

3. The Stoics were a group of philosophers led by Xenon. They got their name from the *stoa* (the porch of the agora) where they met. They believed that nature was controlled by the gods and that if a person simply acted naturally, he could be happy. The Stoics

believed in living calmly and reasonably. Since all men were brothers, they should live together in harmony. The important thing was not to achieve a goal or to change the world, but rather to lead a virtuous life. Today, a stoic is someone who accepts his fate without complaining.

4. Socrates had a brilliant mind, but he did not possess the handsome body portrayed in classical Greek statues. He had a waddling gait, a snub nose, bulging eyes, and a pot belly! Nor was his domestic life ideal. He had a shrewish wife named Xanthippe, and once when he was teased about her nagging behavior he replied, "My great aim in life is to get on well with people. I chose her (Xanthippe) because I knew if I could get on with her I could with anyone!"

Projects:

1. Protagoras was a Sophist (a kind of philosopher) who said that "man is the measure of all things." Find out who the Sophists were and then explain the meaning of this famous statement. How did it challenge the traditional Greek religious beliefs?

2. Diogenes was a philosopher with some unusual ideas. He went barefoot, wore rags, let his hair grow long and walked around with a lantern in the daylight looking for an honest man. He snarled at what others considered proper behavior. Some said that his search for integrity forced him to live like a dog. The Greek word for dog-like is *cynic*. Find out who the Cynics were and what they believed. (Today a cynic is someone whose ideas go against public opinion.)

3. Some philosophers believed that man should spend his time pursuing pleasure (*hedone*). Write a short report about the Hedonists.

4. Epicurus proposed a "comfortable" philosophy. Learn more about it, and compare this approach to life with that of the Stoics.

5. Plato made up an imaginary island for the setting of one of his dialogues. He called it Atlantis. (see page 22) Ever since, people have been trying to find this mysterious island, which supposedly sank into the sea. Was it real or purely fictional? Find out more about Atlantis and present a short report about it to the class.

6. Write a dialogue in which Pericles and Plato argue about what is the best form of government.

Chapter XVII — ALEXANDER THE GREAT

A Disunited Greece

One hundred years after the death of Pericles, the Greek city-states were in a sad state of disarray. Weakened and disillusioned by the long struggles of the Peloponnesian War, they had made no further attempts at confederation. Instead, they bickered and fought with each other over small pieces of land. The glorious vision of Sparta and Athens gallantly leading their countrymen against the invading Persians was but a dim memory, kept alive only in legends and the writings of Herodotus.

Meanwhile, to the north a new power was growing stronger by the day. This was the kingdom of Macedonia, a land of backward, hard-living warriors who, although they spoke a dialect of Greek, were considered barbarians by the more civilized peoples of the long established city-states. Furthermore, the Macedonians were no friends to the Greeks, for they had supported the Persian invaders in the previous century.

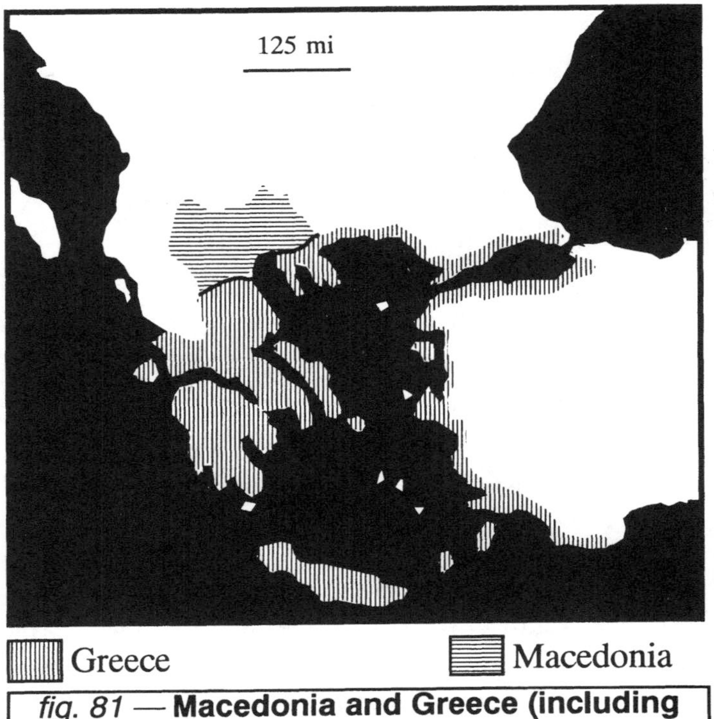

125 mi

Greece   Macedonia

fig. 81 — **Macedonia and Greece (including colonies under Persian control)**

Philip Builds Up His Army

In 359 B.C. Philip II. inherited the throne of Macedonia. He quickly disposed of his rivals and then turned his attention to building up his army.

When he was a boy, Philip had spent time in Thebes as a captive of war. He had carefully studied the phalanxes when they were drilling, and he marveled at the clever tactics of Epaminondas. Now that he was in power, Philip set out to improve upon the formation and strategies of the Theban army in order to make his own forces invincible. He invented a very long (fifteen-foot) spear called the *sarissa* which was carried by the soldiers in the rear ranks of his phalanx. The heavy spear had to be held by two hands, and so a soldier attached his shield to his shoulder with leather straps. He then rested his sarissa upon the shoulder of the man in front of him. The spears were so long that those of the fifth rank protruded through the front line of the phalanx like the quills of a porcupine. This row of pointed spears bristling from flank to flank must have been a frightening sight for any enemy!

To his infantry Philip added a swift moving cavalry. There were few horses in the mountainous lower Greek peninsula, but the gently rolling hills of Macedonia provided excellent pastureland. Sturdy, spirited horses were raised in great numbers there, and Macedonian boys became excellent horsemen at an early age. Philip's cavalry corps was made up of young aristocrats known as the Companions. They made the phalanx more effective than ever before by protecting the flanks and rear of the tightly packed unit of marching men. Under Philip's leadership the Macedonian cavalry became the most renowned horsemen in the ancient Mediterranean world.

Patriotism played an important role in the new army. At a time when the Greek city-states depended more and more upon mercenary soldiers (the local citizens no longer felt the old loyalty to their homeland), Philip built up a well-disciplined, extremely loyal organization of warriors.

Philip greatly respected the rich culture that had flourished in Athens, and he longed to unify all of Greece with his own kingdom. He knew that his timing was right, for the city-states were so busy squabbling with each other that they took no notice of his steady build-up of troops. Whenever he could, Philip encouraged dissension among the Greek states to further divert attention from his military plans. Then he invaded the Greek cities that lay between Macedonia and the coast of the Aegean so that he could gain access to the port cities. When Athens protested, Philip agreed to withdraw his men, but when the protests died down he conveniently forgot his promises to respect Greek boundaries.

Philip Marches South

At last he was ready to begin his attack upon the major cities of Greece. Too late the Greek armies recognized the strength of the Macedonian forces, and Philip systematically subdued them one by one. At Chaeronea he handily defeated the Athenian troops, and this victory ended the Greek resistance, at least for the time being. Philip then organized the Greek city-states into the "Hellenic League." He piously referred to himself as "protector" of the league, for he was keenly aware of the Greeks' disdain for kings. He was determined to win the respect and support of the people he had conquered, not their anger. Each polis was allowed to retain its own local government, but the Greeks had to promise not to fight among themselves or to try to overthrow him. To no one's surprise, Sparta refused to join the league.

Philip's plan was to incorporate the Greek soldiers into his Macedonian army and then march eastward to battle the Persians. His goal was to win back the Ionian cities that had been in Persian hands since the end of the Peloponnesian War. Under his guidance and military might, the old Athenian empire could well be restored, but this time it would be controlled by Macedonia.

The Young Alexander

Philip had several wives. His first wife, Olympias, bore him a son named Alexander. Since Philip was anxious to bring Athenian culture to Macedonia, it was logical for him to choose the learned philosopher Aristotle to tutor his young son (Aristotle, in fact, had grown up in Macedonia). Alexander was a bright and imaginative student, and he was enraptured by Aristotle's reading of THE ILIAD. The boy never tired of hearing the exciting stories about the heroic age of Agamemnon and Menelaus. Achilles became his hero. He dreamed of one day becoming as brave a warrior as that gallant Greek champion who had slain Hector at Troy. Throughout the rest of his life, Alexander always slept with a copy of THE ILIAD under his pillow (as well as a dagger!).

Aristotle also instilled in his pupil an appreciation for the natural environment, and he encouraged him to be open to new ideas and unfamiliar situations. This lesson would serve Alexander well on the battlefield, as we shall see. The young prince came to love Greek art and poetry, and, like his father, he firmly believed that Athenian culture represented the height of all human endeavor.

Bucephalus

As Alexander grew older, he proved himself an excellent horseman. There is a famous story about how Alexander tamed the black stallion that he was to ride for most of his life. According to the legend, a horse trader once brought a very high-spirited animal to sell to Philip. No one could handle the stallion, who reared and bolted whenever someone tried to mount him. The observant prince watched attentively, and then he asked his father if he might have a try with the horse. Philip could not imagine his son succeeding where grown men had failed, but he admired his son's spirit and so he agreed to the request. Alexander (following the advice of Aristotle to observe everything closely) had noticed that the horse shied whenever he saw his own shadow. Therefore, he gathered the reins and gently led the horse toward the sun; then he scrambled aboard and galloped off in that direction. Since there was no shadow, the horse showed no fear and was easily controlled; now that he had

mastered the animal, the boy was able to guide him back to where his father stood. Philip cried tears of joy when he saw his son's accomplishment, and he exclaimed, "Alexander, you must find another kingdom to rule, for Macedonia is surely too small for you!"

Philip gave his son the horse, which was named Bucephalus (meaning "bull head"). No one could ever control the spirited beast except Alexander, for whom he became as docile as a lamb. Bucephalus would lower his great head so that his young master could more easily mount him.

Philip made his son a member of the cavalry when he turned sixteen. Even at this early age Alexander won the respect of the Macedonian horsemen by his skill and boldness in battle. When Philip's army invaded Greece, Alexander (and Bucephalus!) led one wing of the cavalry, while his father commanded the other. Together they led the Macedonian army to victory.

The Death of Philip

Philip's dream to win back the Ionian cities from the Persians was not to be. While attending the wedding of his daughter he was stabbed in the back. The year was 336 B.C. No one knows who planned the murder. Most scholars suspect that his jealous first

fig. 82 — **Alexander and Bucephalus**

wife Olympias was behind the plot. Others suspect the Persians. Some even suspect Alexander. But regardless of who was responsible for Philip's death, his son suddenly found himself king of Macedonia and Greece at the tender age of twenty.

The Greeks were relieved to hear of Philip's death, for they assumed that Alexander could quickly be driven out of their homeland. The boy didn't seem much of a threat. He was only five feet six inches tall, and his clean shaven face and flowing blond hair underscored his youth. But Alexander was supremely confident in his ability to command. He had inherited the ambition and organizational genius of his father, and he was willing to take risks to achieve his goals. Furthermore, he was loyally supported by the Macedonian army.

*fig. 83 — **Alexander***

Alexander Proves His Mettle

Alexander moved swiftly: He imprisoned the Greek leaders who were plotting against him, and he claimed Philip's title for himself. Then he marched north to put down a revolt by tribesmen in Illyria, a rugged territory controlled by the Macedonians. When a rumor circulated in Greece that Alexander had been killed in battle, the city-states (led by Thebes) organized a rebellion against the occupying Macedonian troops. Alexander immediately returned to Greece and defeated the rebellious armies. Philip's long sarissa spears and the aggressive cavalry charge of the Companions easily overwhelmed the Theban phalanxes.

The young king decided to make Thebes an example of what might happen to any Greek polis that resisted him. He destroyed the city, sparing only the house of the poet Pindar, whose verses he had studied with Aristotle and greatly admired. Twenty thousand Thebans who survived the assault were sent into slavery.

Across the Hellespont Into Asia

Once he had regained control of Greece and those Macedonian provinces that had rebelled, Alexander set out to

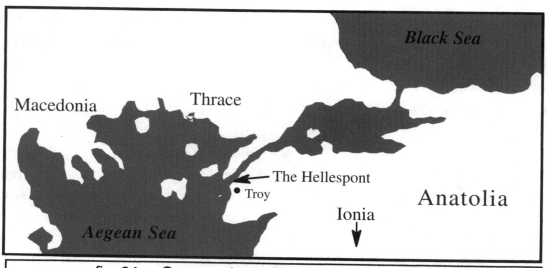

fig. 84 — Greece, the Hellespont and Asia Minor

accomplish his father's goal; the liberation of the Ionian cities. He crossed the Hellespont, just as Xerxes had done over a century before, leading nearly forty thousand Macedonian and Greek soldiers. (Only Sparta did not contribute troops to his army.) He would never return to Europe.

Alexander As the Heir of Achilles

While the ships bearing his troops landed on the Asian coast, Alexander sailed south. Ever the romantic, he had the burning desire to retrace Agamemnon's path to Troy. Once ashore, he set out for the ancient walled city, dramatically quoting passages of THE ILIAD to his comrades as he marched. (Thanks to Aristotle, he had memorized the entire epic!)

When he arrived at Troy, Alexander placed a wreath upon the grave of Achilles and made a sacrifice at the temple of Athena. Bowing his head at the altar, he vowed to finally end the struggle between Europe and Asia that had begun so many years before when (according to Homer) Paris abducted Helen. The Greeks, of course, were to be the ultimate victors. He removed an ancient shield from the temple which he would later carry into battle for good luck.

The Battle At Granicus

Alexander then rejoined his men, and they soon came face to face with the enemy at the Granicus River. The local Persian satrap had placed a line of cavalry along the far shore of the river backed up by a phalanx of mercenaries (hired fighters).

Alexander carefully studied the enemy formation; then he ordered his men into position (the footsoldiers flanked by the cavalry). Suddenly he charged, leading the Companions at a full gallop across the river and up the steep bank on the other side. He moved with such speed and decisiveness that the Persian horsemen were caught off guard; the Companions easily smashed through the enemy line and began hand to hand combat. Alexander was nearly finished off by a Persian cavalryman who attacked him from behind, but his boyhood friend, a dark-bearded man named Cleitus, saved his life by literally slicing off the Persian's arm—sword and all!

The Macedonian footsoldiers then waded across the shallow river and pushed the enemy into retreat with their solid line of spears. It was a glorious day for Alexander! After the battle, he sent three hundred sets of captured Persian armor to the Athenians as tokens of his victory, along with the message that he owed his success to the Greek allies "except the Spartans" (a reference belying his contempt for the red-cloaked warriors who had refused to join his campaign).

The Gordian Knot

From the Granicus Alexander marched southwest to free the Ionian cities. He then moved northeast to Gordium, the capital of the ancient kingdom of Phrygia. According to legend, the yoke of the chariot of a former king named Gordias was tied by an intricately knotted rope (known as the Gordian knot) to a post outside a temple of Zeus. Everyone in the kingdom knew the prophecy connected with the knot: The man who could untie it would conquer all of Asia. For Alexander the temptation must have been irresistible! He cautiously approached the yoke and studied the knot. Then, deciding that he could not untie it, he quickly drew his sword and sliced through it. In his mind he had succeeded in the task, for had he not disposed of the knot and freed the yoke from the post? This episode vividly illustrates the way Alexander typically dealt with a challenge: After carefully examining the principle aspects of the problem, he would spring to action and decisively resolve it. And, as we shall see, the prophecy of the Gordian Knot would indeed be fulfilled. Today, "to untie the Gordian Knot" means to solve a difficult problem quickly and decisively.

The Battle of Issus

As Alexander moved south from Gordium, a huge Persian army assembled. The king of Persia at this time was Darius III. He had come to power the very same year as Alexander. As we know, the Persians always referred to their monarch as the Great King, and Darius certainly lived up to the image, at least physically. He was a very tall man for those early times (at a towering 6'6" he was a foot taller than Alexander), and his full black beard made him appear virile and all-powerful. Darius was a proud and haughty man. There was some cause for his arrogance: He ruled an empire covering two million square miles!

The Persian force was massive (the number of Greek mercenaries serving under Darius alone equalled the size of Alexander's entire army). Like a dreaded behemoth, it slowly advanced to meet the Greeks at Issus, Syria. But Alexander wasn't too worried. He figured that its vast size and lack of discipline would make the Persian army unwieldy, and he had also heard stories about the indecisive (some said cowardly) personality of Darius. Issus was a narrow plain between the sea and the mountains, and its restricted space prevented Darius from using all of his troops. So when he scanned the ranks of enemy soldiers facing him, Alexander looked for a weakness; suddenly he saw a gap in the front line. It was a moment for quick action! Alexander charged at a full gallop, leading his lightning-fast Companions through the gap, followed by the tightly-knit phalanx of soldiers wielding their long metal-tipped sarissas.

When Darius caught a glimpse of Alexander skillfully guiding Buchephalus toward him, a gleaming sword raised above his head, the cowardly Persian king panicked and fled the battle in his golden chariot! This unexpected desertion by the king left his army in utter confusion, and thousands of Persian troops were trampled by their fellow soldiers.

Darius also abandoned his mother, wife and daughters, who were waiting anxiously in a camp nearby. Alexander made the women his prisoners, but he treated them with chivalry and respect. He was disgusted that "the Great King" had deserted his family, and he couldn't imagine why he had brought them so dangerously near the field of battle in the first place. When Alexander entered Darius' abandoned tent, he was dazzled by the priceless jewels, gold and silver tableware, inlaid furniture, golden throne and elaborate bath tub set up there. As he triumphantly sat down to the feast that had been prepared for the Persian monarch, he exclaimed, "So this is what it is like to be king!" It was his first encounter with the luxuries of the East.

Meanwhile, Darius was anxious for peace at any price, and so he sent ambassadors to Alexander offering a rich ransom as well as most of Anatolia. Alexander staunchly refused the offer, saying that he would not be paid off with land that he had already won. When Parmenio, one of his generals, suggested, "I would accept this if I were Alexander," the young king disdainfully replied, "and so would I, if I were Parmenio!" Clearly Alexander's ambition was greater than that of his subordinate.

Alexander Gains Control of the Coast

After the stunning victory at Issus, the Greek army swept south along the Mediterranean coast of Asia. Alexander worried that Darius might receive support from his fleet of ships, and so he decided to cut off communications between the Persian sea and land forces. With this goal in mind, he conquered the territories of Phoenicia and Palestine; then he moved south to besiege the island port city of Tyre (a

Phoenician city controlled by Persia). The siege lasted for seven months, but Alexander finally destroyed the city by building a bridge of stone and cedar beams across the mile-wide channel separating Tyre from the mainland. Across this bridge his men dragged catapults and siege towers for a final assault of the island fortress. With this

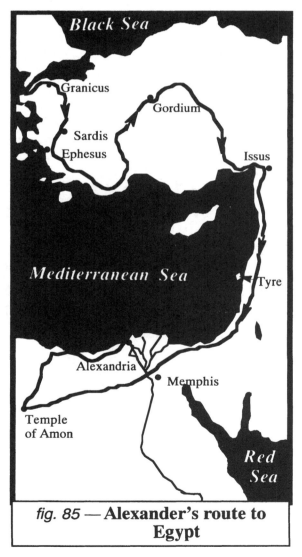

fig. 85 — **Alexander's route to Egypt**

victory, Alexander could claim control of the entire eastern Mediterranean coast.

Sojourn In Egypt

In 332 B.C. Alexander entered Egypt. This rich civilization that had flourished for nearly three thousand years had been conquered by the Persians in the sixth century B.C. The Egyptian people hated their foreign masters, and they joyously welcomed Alexander as their liberator and the rightful ruler of their nation.

Alexander always respected foreign customs, and he knew that religion lay at the heart of Egyptian culture. Therefore, soon after his arrival in Egypt he set out for the ancient city of Memphis to offer sacrifices to the Egyptian gods.

The young conqueror had so enjoyed learning about the natural world with Aristotle that he brought several scientists along with him on his long journey. He frequently sent specimens of plant life back to his former teacher, who now lived in Athens. While in Egypt, Alexander dispatched a party of men to Nubia (modern Sudan) to discover the cause of the annual flooding of the Nile; they reported that the heavy spring rains in the mountains to the southeast combined with the melting snow caused the river to flood its banks. Until then, the Egyptians believed the yearly inundation was an act of the gods!

As Alexander walked about the ancient tombs and temples that line the Nile, he must have been reexamining his reasons for leading an army across two continents. His ambitions had certainly grown since he first crossed the Hellespont. He now controlled not only Ionia but Egypt and the western coast of Asia as well. It was clear that his military capabilities were extra-ordinary—what new conquests could they lead to? Alexander was fascinated by the Asian and African cultures he had encountered, and perhaps he pondered ruling an empire made up of a diversity of peoples. Or maybe he simply craved power.

The expanding empire needed a centrally located city to coordinate trade in the eastern Mediterranean. The coast of Egypt seemed the ideal location, and Alexander selected a site in the Nile delta overlooking a protected harbor. Kneeling on the sand, he drew with a reed his plan for the city: The streets were to be arranged in a grid, and there would be temples, government buildings, markets and places for scholars to gather and study. Of course, the city would be named Alexandria (many Alexandrias were to be founded throughout the young king's travels, but this one was destined for greatness). Alexander appointed an architect named Dinocrates to oversee the construction of the city, but he would not live to see its completion.

From there he crossed the scorching sands of the western desert to visit the oasis of Siwa, the site of the holy shrine of the god Amon. The priests of Amon's temple acknowledged Alexander as the legitimate Pharaoh (king of Egypt); since the Egyptians considered their Pharaoh a living god, Alexander now held a divine status. He must have enjoyed this new role! Coins made soon after this time show him wearing ram horns, the symbol of Amon.

fig. 86 — A coin showing Alexander with a ram's horns

The Battle of Gaugamela

Alexander remained in Egypt for six months. But he knew that Darius was waiting for him, and so he returned to Asia, leading his troops across the Euphrates River to the banks of the Tigris in Mesopotamia (modern Iraq) for a final showdown.

At Gaugamela the Persian king had assembled an army even larger than the one he led at Issus (his troops now outnumbered the Greeks five to one!), and he had a secret device; fifty war chariots with deadly scythe blades attached to their wheels. The Great King planned to use these gruesome vehicles to literally cut through the Greek phalanx!

Alexander spent the night before the battle carefully studying the layout of the field and planning his strategy. The next day he placed lightly-armed footsoldiers in front of his phalanx. When the chariots charged, these agile men jumped aside to avoid the blades and then hurled their javelins at the charioteers. Then the phalanx split in two, allowing the horses to draw the empty chariots through the gap. Once that obstacle had been dealt with, Alexander led the Companions and the infantry in a swift attack against the Persian line. Remembering Darius's cowardly nature, he galloped directly toward the Great King; as expected, Darius turned tail and fled! When the Persian soldiers realized that they had once again been deserted by their leader, they lost heart and retreated. Darius was later assassinated by his own bodyguard.

Alexander Reaches the Heart of the Persian Empire

The victorious Greeks marched from Gaugamela to the ancient city of Babylon, where the people quickly surrendered without any bloodshed (see the map on p. 188). Alexander honored the local gods and ordered the restoration of the sacred Babylonian shrines that had been damaged by the Persians. Then he continued on to Susa, where he gleefully helped himself to the sacks full of gold coins lying in Darius's royal vaults. He sent many of the coins back to the Greek city-state of Platea, because its soldiers had fought so bravely during the Persian War.

It was winter, but in spite of the bad weather, Alexander led his men over the mountains to Persepolis, the capital of the Persian empire and the site of its rich central treasury (worth half a billion dollars!). The local soldiers hadn't expected an invasion at that time of the year, and so he met little resis-tance. Alexander later assembled caravans using 20,000 mules and 5,000 camels to carry the golden treasure back to Greece.

By now his men desperately needed a rest, and so Alexander spent the rest of the winter in Persepolis. But after many weeks of luxurious living, this pleasant interlude came to an abrupt end when Darius's beautiful palace (in which Alexander was living) burned to the ground. Alexander was unhurt. No one is certain why the palace was destroyed, but some scholars believe that Alexander ordered its destruction in revenge for Xerxes' burning of Athens over a century earlier. Others suggest that he was drinking heavily with his generals and that he (or someone else) simply started the fire "for kicks."

After the fire, Alexander's thoughts turned back to his empire. He was now master of Persia and incredibly rich. He could have returned to Macedonia. Instead, he marched east to consolidate the distant regions of what had become his empire. He battled many tribal warriors, but they were no match for the Greek army. It seemed to everyone that Alexander was invincible, and in military matters he certainly was: In his lifetime he never lost a single battle!

The New Great King

As Alexander piled up victory after victory, his men noticed a change in his attitude and demeanor; some worried that he was turning into a Persian. Indeed, the new Great King began to wear the purple robes of Persian royalty, and he even married an Asian princess, Roxanne (some say she was his one true love). And his decision to hire Persian mercenaries was viewed by his men as a tremendous insult; they thought it was wrong to dilute the Greek ranks of the army with foreigners (especially former enemies). But a greater blow was yet to come. Intrigued by the court etiquette of the Asians, Alexander decided to adopt many local royal customs; particularly offensive to his men was his insistence that they kneel before him. The Greeks had never treated their leaders in such an idolatrous manner (nor even their gods, for that matter), and they refused to do so now. Alexander did not press the issue and later abandoned the idea, but the old feeling of comraderie and mutual support that he had shared with his men in the early days was waning.

The Death of An Old Friend

The growing uneasiness erupted into violence one night when Alexander was drinking heavily with his generals. Cleitus, the soldier who had saved Alexander's life at Granicus, proposed a toast to Philip, crediting him with the Greek victories in Asia because he had created the Macedonian army in the first place. Alexander, drunk and angered by not receiving full credit for his successes, seized a spear and fatally stabbed his old friend. He later regretted what he had done, but his men never forgave him.

Perhaps in an effort to cast off his feelings of guilt, Alexander ordered his men to prepare for yet another march. This time they headed northeast across a rugged terrain until they reached a river in Russia that supposedly marked the end of the world; another city (Alexandria the Farthest) was founded there. As he had done every time he conquered or established a city, Alexander left behind a number of his men to serve as governors and to introduce the ideals and principles of Greek culture to the local people. Then he headed south.

Onward Into India

In 327 B.C. Alexander's army crossed the western part of the towering Himalayan Mountains (the Hindu Kush). The scientists in his party charted the areas they crossed, and their maps were to be of great value to later

Europeans' understanding of the geography of Asia.

In those days the Greeks believed that India was a small peninsula whose eastern shores were washed by a vast body of water called Ocean (the all-encircling Ocean that we learned about in Chapter IX). For this reason, Alexander was convinced that once he reached the eastern coast of India his empire would extend to the end of the earth. It was an exciting possibility!

An Encounter With King Porus

On the far side of the Hindu Kush stretched the wide plain of the Punjab. The Indus River cuts through the plain on its way to the Indian Ocean. It was here that Alexander faced his most difficult battle. An army that included two hundred war elephants was waiting for him on the far shore of the river. Its

fig. 87 — **A war elephant**

leader, a local monarch named Porus, was mounted on one of the largest elephants. Porus himself was a tall man (some say he was seven feet tall!) and he was a shrewd and courageous adversary.

Alexander devised a strategy for dealing with the elephants. He ordered his light infantry to throw their spears at the drivers riding atop the huge beasts and to prod the animals with their daggers. The plan worked fairly well, and many of the elephants panicked and trampled the Indian foot-soldiers. But Porus' men fought on with such determination and skill that the battle lasted for hours.

When the fighting was over Alexander had won—but it was to be his last great battle. King Porus was taken prisoner, and when Alexander asked him how he expected to be treated, the proud monarch responded, "Like a king!" When Alexander asked what he meant, Porus replied that his words expressed everything. Alexander was always impressed by men who showed personal courage and dignity, and so he restored to Porus his kingdom, with the understanding that it would be ruled as a part of his own empire.

Alexander's last battle coincided with the death of his faithful steed

Bucephalus. The gallant black stallion who had carried his master thousands of miles finally died of the accumulated effects of his war wounds and old age. Alexander was greatly saddened by the loss of Bucephalus, and he buried him with great pomp and ceremony. He founded a city (Bucephala) at the site of the stallion's grave.

The End of the Road

Alexander continued marching eastward, determined to reach the waters of Ocean. But his men were exhausted, and they were dispirited by rumors that there was yet another great river (the Ganges) to cross before they reached India's eastern shoreline. Many of them had followed their king faithfully for nearly 3,000 miles, but now they refused to take another step. They begged him to return home.

Alexander moped in his tent for three days (just as Achilles had done in THE ILIAD), and then he finally acknowledged that he had no choice but to turn back. He insisted, however, that he return by a different route than he had come. To do otherwise would imply a retreat. Besides, he was eager to explore new territories and perhaps conquer more land.

A Difficult March

He divided his forces, sending one group by boat to the mouth of the Indus River from whence it would proceed westward along the coast to the Persian Gulf. Two other groups marched by land, one of them led by Alexander. His return trip was the most difficult part of the entire journey. After reaching the mouth of the river and following the southern coast of India, he came to some mountains and was forced to march inland through a scorching desert. Supplies quickly ran out, and the starving troops had to slaughter the baggage animals in order to survive. Nor was it easy to find the way. The staggering soldiers frequently got lost in the blowing desert sands. They marched at night to avoid the blistering heat of the sun, but they did not always escape the hazards of flash floods, poisonous snakes or hostile tribesmen.

As ever, Alexander shared the hardships of his men. He sent his own horse to the rear and marched on foot with his troops, refusing water when there was not enough for everyone. The trek homeward was a nightmare. During the sixty-day march thousands of his men died of thirst, starvation, and heat stroke.

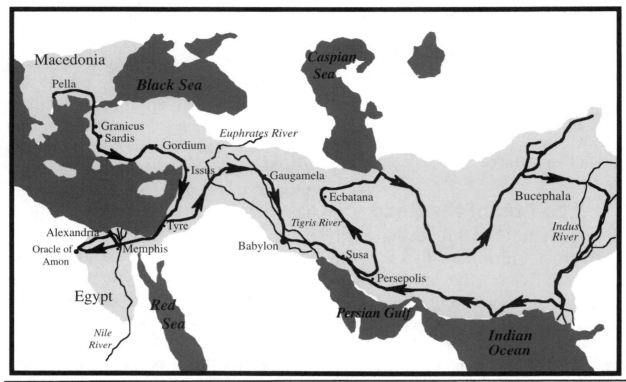

fig. 88 — Alexander's march

A Return to Babylon

When they finally arrived in Susa, the surviving soldiers eagerly consumed large quantities of water and then collapsed from utter exhaustion. When he and his men recovered their strength, Alexander moved on to Babylon; there he punished the corrupt local officials who had taken advantage of his absence and then reorganized the city government.

Alexander had now begun to seriously think of himself as a Greco-Persian, and he probably dreamed of ruling a multinational empire founded upon the Greek way of life. To symbolize the mingling of Greek and Persian cultures, he ordered his soldiers to marry Asian women in a mass ceremony; he himself married two of the daughters of Darius. Soon afterwards, Alexander arranged for 30,000 Persian youths to begin military training under Macedonian instructors.

Most of Alexander's men did not share his vision of a Greco-Persian society, and they continued to complain about diluting their ranks with "barbarian" blood. More and more they questioned their leader's sanity. There seemed good cause for this when Alexander announced that he should henceforth be recognized as the son of Zeus-Amon (a deity having the attributes of the Greek god Zeus and the Egyptian god Amon). Did he actually believe the words of the priests at Siwa? When news of his proclaimed deification were sent to Greece, the Spartans replied with characteristic understatement, "Let Alexander be a god if he wants to." Apparently, they were not impressed!

The Death of Alexander

Alexander soon grew restless in Babylon, and he began to make plans to conquer Arabia. But this campaign never took place. In June, 323 B.C. he fell ill with a high fever. No one is sure whether he contracted malaria or was poisoned. But whatever the cause, Alexander's hours were numbered. As he lay dying in his tent, his generals gathered around him, wondering who would be in command after he was gone. It was reported that when asked to whom he would leave his great empire, Alexander whispered, "to the strongest."

He died in the thirty-third year of his life. He had ruled for thirteen years and amassed the largest empire the world had ever known. Like his hero Achilles, he had lived a short, glorious life that would be celebrated and remembered for all time.

The Aftermath

Alexander's body was placed in a solid gold coffin. After a funeral in Babylon the coffin was positioned on a wagon beneath a jewel-encrusted golden temple. The wagon was drawn by sixty-four mules wearing golden bells across one thousand miles to Egypt. He was finally laid to rest in the city he had founded years before in the delta of the Nile, Alexandria.

After many years of struggle, Alexander's empire was finally divided among three of his generals. Seleucus ruled the Persian empire east to the Indus River (it was called the Seleucid empire), Antigonus gained control of Macedonia, Greece and Crete, and Ptolemy established a dynasty in Egypt.

Alexander's Legacy

Although Alexander's great empire did not hold together after his death, he did leave a rich legacy. The network of Greek cities he had established became important commercial centers. Greeks living in Europe were attracted by the trading prospects in the new cities and they flocked to inhabit them, taking

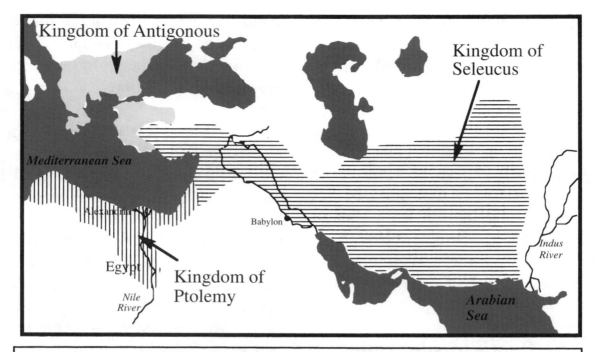

fig. 89 — Alexander's empire divided into three parts

their rich culture with them. Alexander had created a uniform coinage in his empire, and this greatly facilitated trade throughout the Mediterranean world. The Greek language was spoken by educated people in the major cities of his empire (the dialect spoken in Asia was called Koine); even the Christian Bible would be written in Greek. But perhaps Alexander's greatest legacy was that he had broken down many of the barriers between the East and the West and opened up the doors to a multinational sharing of trade, art and political ideals.

Questions:

1. How did Philip improve his army?
2. Who was Alexander's great hero?
3. How did Alexander tame Bucephalus?
4. How did most Greeks react to the news of Philip's death?
5. Why did Alexander win at Granicus?
6. What does it mean to "untie the Gordian Knot?"
7. Describe the physique and personality of Darius the Great.
8. Why did Alexander conquer the ports along the western coast of Asia?
9. How did Alexander show his respect for foreign cultures when he was in Egypt?

10. What was Darius' "lethal weapon" at Issus?

11. Why did Alexander's men become uneasy?

12. Why did Alexander restore to Porus his kingdom?

13. Why was the return from India to Babylon so difficult for Alexander and his men?

14. To whom did Alexander leave his empire?

15. What was Alexander's legacy?

Ideas to Think About

1. Demosthenes was a great orator who tried in vain to warn his fellow Athenians about the danger posed by Philip of Macedonia. He wrote a series of speeches called THE PHILIPPICS, warning that an invasion by Philip would mark the end of democracy. The one time he managed to unite Athens and Thebes against Philip, the Greeks lost to the Macedonians at the battle of Chaeronea. After Philip's death, Demosthenes spoke just as fervently about the danger that Alexander presented. Some people heeded his words, but in general his pleas fell upon deaf ears. Later, when the Macedonians conquered Greece and demanded the execution of Demosthenes, the poor man ended his life by drinking poison.

2. Alexander sought out the famous philosopher Diogenes when he visited Corinth. This highly respected but eccentric philosopher believed that one should separate himself from all unnecessary luxury, and so he lived in a huge barrel, and he carried a lighted lantern by daylight in a never-ending search for an honest man. (see page 163) Diogenes believed in the community of mankind and opposed the idea of independent city states. In fact, he invented the word *cosmolite* which meant "citizen of the world." Perhaps it was he who planted in the young conqueror's mind the idea of a world community. When Alexander came upon Diogenes he asked him if he had anything to say to him. The philosopher replied, "I would ask you to stand out of my light." Alexander, impressed with the confidence and independence of the old man, exclaimed, "If I were not Alexander, I would be Diogenes!"

Some Greek historians wrote that Diogenes died at the age of ninety on the very same day as Alexander, although modern scholars suspect that this coincidence might have been contrived by romantic writers of the past.

3. Alexander had been hunting Darius when he came across the dead body of

the Great King. He threw his cloak over the corpse and sent it back to Persepolis for a royal burial. He did not admire Darius the man, but he greatly respected the traditions of the Persian people.

4. Alexander outgrew the political ideas of his teacher Aristotle. While the old philosopher believed that the city-state must be a self-sufficient unit of civilization, Alexander sought a more open world-wide community. Perhaps it was in part this belief in the autonomy of each city-state that prevented Greece from evolving beyond the Golden Age. Direct democracy worked well in a city-state of 20,000 people, but the Greeks never carried the idea a step further to representative democracy. Had they done so, perhaps Greece could have expanded into the kind of multinational nation that Alexander envisioned.

5. Alexander's great military successes were due in part to his imaginative strategies. Once, when he encountered a very superstitious tribe in Illyria, he ordered his troops to march in precision in absolute silence. Ordinarily, the soldiers sang a war song and marched to the sounds of a double flute. The effect was so eerie that many enemy soldiers dashed off the battlefield in sheer fright!

Projects:

1. It has been said that Alexander embodied the Greek ideal of living life to its fullest. What sacrifices do you think he made because of his love of action? Do you consider his life a full life? Why or why not? Write a short essay expressing your opinion.

2. Find out more about Demosthenes. What did he do to get over his stuttering? Write a short report about this great orator who overcame his physical limitations.

3. Make a timeline showing Alexander's accomplishments.

4. "Alexander was Achilles." Write a short essay explaining why you agree with this statement, or why you don't.

5. The Persian Empire was established by King Cyrus I (Cyrus the Great). He was one of Alexander's heroes. Find out more about Cyrus. Then write an essay, explaining why you think Alexander was drawn to him.

Chapter XVIII — THE HELLENISTIC AGE

A Blending of Cultures

As we know, the Greeks called themselves Hellenes, and so the culture that Alexander helped to spread throughout western Asia and Egypt is called Hellenistic (Greek-like). Those Greeks from the mainland who rushed eastward to take advantage of the trading opportunities in Alexander's new cities strengthened the cultural traditions that had originally been established there by men recruited from Alexander's army. Each city was modeled upon Athens and contained pillared temples and government buildings, an open-air theater, gymnasiums, and a centrally located agora. The architecture was somewhat more ornate than that of the Golden Age, and elaborate Corinthian columns supported the roofs of the buildings. (See a description of Greek pillars on page 122.) A Hellenistic city had a democratic government and observed the traditional Greek religious festivals, but its citizens were also greatly influenced by the cultures of the surrounding areas as well as the new ideas and technologies emanating from the distant Orient. For this reason, the Hellenistic Age that followed Alexander's death can best be described as a blending of Greek and eastern cultures; it lasted for about three hundred years and ended when Augustus became Emperor of Rome.

Alexandria

Alexander had hoped that the city he founded in Egypt would become an international center; during the Hellenistic Age it did indeed become the hub of trade and learning in the Mediterranean world. Although over one half of the city's population was Greek, there were also scholars and merchants from Italy, Crete, Syria, Arabia and even India.

The city stood majestically above the waters of the Nile delta like a beacon of gleaming marble. The streets were laid out in the grid pattern that Alexander had once sketched in the sand. Within its encircling walls were a Hall of Justice, government offices, warehouses and shops, while beyond lay a hippodrome and a stadium. A canal brought water from the Nile, and clay pipes conducted it to the private homes of the wealthy.

Alexandria also had a vast library of over 700,000 volumes written on papyrus; the library was part of a huge temple dedicated to the Muses (nine Greek goddesses believed to inspire such creative activities as poetry and music), and for this reason it was called the Museum. Scholars came there to read and discuss the great works of the age, and the Museum slowly evolved into the ancient equivalent of a modern university. Those who came to Alexandria to study were exempt from taxes, and in some cases the Egyptian government even provided them with a living allowance.

A huge lighthouse (called the Pharos because it was built on the island of Pharas) dominated the city's skyline. Its four hundred-foot tower was crowned by a polished steel mirror that was visible to ships thirty miles away in the Mediterranean Sea. The Pharos was such an impressive structure that it was

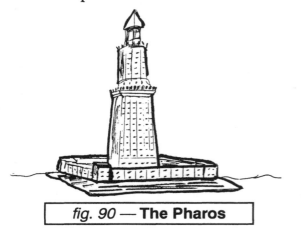

*fig. 90 — **The Pharos***

considered one of the Seven Wonders of the Ancient World. It was destroyed by an earthquake centuries ago. Today the French word for lighthouse is "phare".

Egypt was governed in those days by the Ptolemies, the dynasty established by one of Alexander's generals. The ruling class spoke Greek, worshiped Zeus and drank imported wine rather than the local beer; unfortunately, they also treated the native Egyptians as second-class citizens!

Mainland Greece

After the death of Alexander, Athens declined as a major trading port, but it continued to thrive as a center of study and learning. The other city-states of mainland Greece combined to form two leagues: the Aetolian League (cities north of the Isthmus of Corinth) and the Achaean League (the Peloponnese). Indeed, Greece was now better unified than it had ever been in the past, but the days of glory were over.

Hellenistic Art

The Greek artists of the Hellenistic period found that their works were greatly in demand. The new cities in Asia needed statues for their temples, parks and private gardens. Furthermore, it became fashionable among the rich throughout the Mediterranean world to have their portraits chiseled in stone. The sculptors in Athens and other mainland cities could not keep up with the demand, and eventually factories were set up near the quarries to speed up what became the mass production of statues. Boatloads of them were then shipped to all the major ports. Life-like statues were also molded in pottery; many of these had interchangeable heads so that a customer could order a particular facial expression and the appropriate head would be placed atop a "generic" clay body!

Most Hellenistic statues differ from the classical figures of the Golden Age. The earlier statues portray the idealized human body and create a feeling of restraint and detachment; the Hellenistic figures are realistic, and they often depict more violent emotion. Rather than sculpt a handsome young athlete, the Hellenistic artist was likely to portray a wrinkled old woman or a dying soldier. A famous statue of this period is called "The Laocoön." This work graphically portrays a Trojan priest and his two sons in a final, agonizing death struggle against a huge, undulating serpent. (Laocoon had warned the Trojans not to take the wooden horse into the city.)

The influence of Greek art spread

*fig. 91 — **The Laocoön***

as far as India, where the surviving statues of Buddha that were sculpted at this time bear a striking resemblance to Apollo!

Hellenistic Religions

The Greeks who lived in Alexander's new cities continued to worship the Olympian gods and to participate in the religious festivals. Yet, their exposure to the religions of the East made them increasingly aware of the limitations of the old Greek religion. We learned earlier that there was no moral code connected with the worship of the Olympian gods and goddesses. One of the major functions of religious traditional activities had been to bring the people together, and the sacrifices were offered to obtain favors from particular deities. But the Greek religion offered no inspiration to the people to lead a better life, nor did it address the important issues of sin, personal redemption, and immortality.

Some Greeks who sought a more mystical religious experience had been drawn to the cults associated with certain gods. The mystery cult of Eleusis, for example, evolved from a worship of the goddess Demeter and her daughter Persephone. It focused upon the natural cycle of the growing season, and implied that, like the farmer's crops, a human life could be reborn in another world. Members of the cult had to pass special tests before being accepted, and then they were sworn to secrecy, so we know little about their activities. We do know that they experienced a feeling of communication with the deities through highly emotional mass rituals. (Of course, such emotional outpourings ran counter to the Greek standard of logic and reason!)

During the Hellenistic Age the need for a mystical experience was often fulfilled by the religions that had flourished for centuries in the lands conquered by Alexander. The Egyptian goddess Isis appealed to many Greek women, and the Persian god Mithras was a popular deity among soldiers. In Alexandria a new god known as Serapis was invented by Ptolemy. Serapis embodied elements of the Egyptian god Osiris and the Greek gods Zeus, Apollo, and Hades. He promised virtuous people eternal life.

The Greek Language and Literature

Greek became the international language of diplomacy, literature and science throughout Alexander's former empire. Centuries later the New Testament of the Bible would be written in Greek.

The colorful gods and goddesses of Mt. Olympus lived on in art, drama and poetry written during this period, but nature was also the subject of many important works. Theocritus, a Greek who lived for some time in Alexandria, wrote beautiful poems about the simple country life of Arcadia. Meleager wrote fascinating epigrams and inspiring love poems. Both Theocritus and Meleager had a strong influence upon later Roman and British poets.

The greatest achievements of the Hellenistic Age were in the field of science and technology, and we shall learn about them in the following chapter.

Questions:

1. What does "Hellenistic" mean?
2. How did the Greeks living in Alexandria treat the Egyptians?
3. What was the Museum?
4. How did the Greek art of the Hellenistic Period differ from that of the Golden Age?
5. Why did foreign religious cults appeal to many Greeks?
6. Who was Theocritus?

Ideas to Think About:

1. Although Alexandria was a center for scholars during the Hellenistic period, Athens never lost her reputation as a place of learning. Aristotle's school, the Lyceum, continued to thrive for a century after his death. Many of the leading families of Egypt, Asia and later Rome sent their children to Athens to be educated.

2. Greek and Latin were the common languages of scholars of all nations until quite recently. And think about the names of such categories as the species of plants and animals, chemical elements and compounds, and the medicines on the shelf in the neighborhood drugstore. In the scientific community, Greek and Latin words still form the basis of a universal language.

Projects:

1. Find a detailed description of Alexandria in a book in the library. Using clay or paper mache, make a diorama of the city. Include such structures as the lighthouse, museum, and hippodrome, and show the grid pattern of the streets.

2. Find a book about ancient and classical art in your library. Then select two Greek statues that are shown in the book, one that was made during the Golden Age and one dating from the Hellenistic Age. Study the pictures carefully, and read any text that concerns them. Then write a short report comparing and contrasting the two statues. Be sure to tell which statue you prefer (and why).

3. Find out more about Theocritus or Meleager, and write a short report.

4. Callimachus was a Greek poet best known for the line, "They told me, Heraclitus, they told me you were dead." Find out more about this writer of the Hellenistic Age, and present a short report.

Chapter XIX — GREEK ADVANCES IN SCIENCE

The Early Discoveries

As a race, the Greeks were extremely inquisitive about the make-up and functioning of the natural world, but the greatest advances in scientific knowledge were made beyond the shores of the mainland in the Aegean islands, Ionia, southern Italy, and, of course, Alexandria. It was in those bustling trading centers that ideas as well as products were constantly exchanged, and the scholars living there were able to freely embrace new concepts and then use them to make dramatic discoveries of their own.

Thales of Miletus

Thales of Miletus was the first great Greek philosopher; he lived in the seventh century B.C. in the Ionian seaport that was later destroyed by the Persians. Remember, the word "philosopher" originally referred to anyone who enjoyed studying things. Thales was primarily interested in astronomy and mathematics, and his curiosity about the measurement of distances took him to Egypt. There he studied the structures of the pyramids and thought about the rules of geometry that had been applied to build them. He noticed that at a certain time of day a man's shadow is equal to his height, and he used this principle to measure the height of the Great Pyramid. Can you explain how he did it?

Thales also studied eclipses of the sun, and according to legend he even predicted one successfully. He was greatly impressed by the relatively efficient 365-day calendar used by the Egyptians, and he introduced it to the Greeks. Our own calendar is based upon it.

Thales' most important contribution to science was his theory that the world had been formed by a natural process and was not the creation of the gods. Furthermore, he proposed that nature was governed by certain unchanging laws, and he said that human beings could discover these laws by carefully observing their environment. Thales was the first Greek to write about the science of nature (*physis*), and his attempt to understand and explain the origin of life using scientific rather than religious evidence marked an important break with the past. He did not question, however, the traditional belief that the earth was a flat disc floating upon an all-encircling ocean.

The Theories of Anaximander

Anaximander was a pupil of Thales. After years of studying the heavens, he concluded that the the earth had been produced by a huge explosion. He also proposed that the sun, moon and stars moved in circles around the earth, a theory that would be supported by most scientists for two millennia. Anaximander observed the creatures of the earth, and he concluded that the first living things lived in the water and that over time some of these creatures learned to live on the land; it was from them that human beings evolved. His theory seemed to be confirmed when a later scholar, Xenophanes, examined some fossils and decided that they were the remains of plants and animals that had lived millions of years ago preserved in rock. These observations, made over two thousand years ago, form the basis of the modern science of evolution.

Anaximander also drew the earliest known map of the world upon a brass tablet. Not surprisingly, Greece lies in the center of the map, attached to the rest of Europe and separated by the sea from Asia. Of course, the land is entirely surrounded by water (Ocean). In the sixth century B.C. Hecataeus revised the world map to include northern Africa (which he labeled as part of Asia).

The Atomic Theory

Other Greek scholars tried to ascertain the basic components of the universe. And what was the single substance from which everything else had evolved? Was it liquid or gas? Scientific investigation was in its infancy at this time, and yet revolutionary discoveries did take place. An Ionian named Democritus came to the conclusion that all things are made up of tiny particles called atoms, an amazingly accurate deduction in a time when there were no scientific instruments!

Pythagoras

Pythagoras was a philosopher born near Miletus who traveled extensively in Europe, Asia and Africa and then settled in Crotona, a Greek colony in southern Italy. (Crotona was the birthplace of Milo, the champion of the pancratium—see page 109). There he founded a school to study geometry, arithmetic, astronomy and music. His school accepted women students as well as men—an astonishing innovation in the strongly male-oriented Greek society. Pythagoras knew something about right triangles from a rule of geometry that the Egyptians had used to make the corners of their buildings square. According to this rule, if a triangle has sides which are three, four and five units long respectively, the angle between the two shorter sides is a right angle (90 degrees). Pythagoras used this knowledge to make a new rule: In a right triangle the area of the square on the longest side equals the sum of the areas (squares) of the other two sides (A square is the distance between two points times itself.). This is called the Pythagorian Theorem, and it is one of the basic rules of modern geometry. He also discovered that the sum of the angles within any triangle equals two right angles.

Pythagoras believed that ours is an orderly universe whose center is the earth. He was the first person to call the earth round and to refer to the universe as "cosmos" (a Greek word meaning order). He loved mathematics and proposed that the arrangement of the universe could be expressed in numbers. He later experimented with music and discovered the numerical ratio between the length of the string of an instrument and the note it produces. A shorter string produces a higher pitch than a longer one. He also observed that the sounds produced by different strings are especially harmonious when the lengths of the strings are in a certain numerical proportion to one another, such as three to two or four to five. Based upon his findings Pythagoras created a seven note musical scale.

Despite their great strides in scientific discovery, the Greeks remained a superstitious people. Pythagoras himself believed in reincarnation (the concept that the soul of a dead person was passed on to the body of another creature in which it was reborn). He told his students that he could clearly remember his own past lives, including the time he fought in the Trojan War.

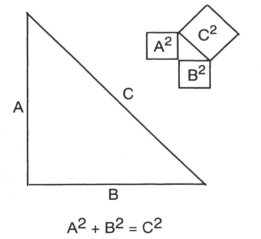

$$A^2 + B^2 = C^2$$

fig. 92 — **The Pythagorian Theorem**

The Heliocentric Theory

Anaxagoras was the teacher of Pericles and later (possibly) Socrates. He proposed that the moon did not produce its own light, but rather that it reflected the light of the sun. He wrote that the sun was a red hot stone "considerably larger than the Peloponnese." Like Thales, he studied eclipses, and he proposed that they were caused by the moon passing between the earth and the sun, blocking the light.

Aristarchus was an astronomer who was educated at Aristotle's Lyceum. He accurately measured the size of the sun and the moon, and he calculated their distance from earth. His estimate of the length of a year (the time it takes the earth to circle the sun) was only seven minutes and sixteen seconds too short! He argued against Aristotle's view that the earth is the center of the universe, instead proposing that the moon, earth and planets move around the sun. This is called the heliocentric theory. Unfortunately, the people of the ancient world were accustomed to the belief that the earth was the center of all things, and they scoffed at his idea that our planet was but one of many heavenly bodies circling the sun. The heliocentric theory would not be accepted by the scientific community until the sixteenth century A.D.

Aristotle

We have already learned about Aristotle's accomplishments in the field of science. He was one of the earliest proponents of the scientific method: He closely observed an aspect of the natural world, analyzed his findings and then carefully recorded his conclusions. He classified over five hundred animals, and he was the first to observe that dolphins were not fish but mammals because they give birth to live offspring. Aristotle also studied the development of chick embryos and drew detailed charts documenting the changes that occurred. (He preserved the embryos in honey!)

Aristotle's work in natural science was carried on by Theophrastus, who later became the head of the Lyceum. Theophrastus analyzed the specimens and data made available by Alexander during his marches through Asia. After his death, the focus of scientific research would move from Athens to Alexandria.

Advances of the Hellenistic Age

The Hellenistic Age marked the high point of scientific research and discovery in the ancient world. The surge of intellectual activity was spurred on by the common language spoken throughout Alexander's empire that enabled scholars of different cultures to share their knowledge. Another contributing factor was the weakening of traditional religious beliefs.

One of the great mathematicians of the time was a Greek named Euclid who founded a school in Alexandria. He wrote a series of textbooks (THE ELEMENTS) which describe the specific steps that must be followed to solve different kinds of problems in geometry. Euclid is called the Father of Geometry and his works form the basis of modern geometry texts.

Further Progress in Geometry

Eratosthenes was the chief librarian of the Museum at Alexandria. In his book about geography he described the world as a sphere. His estimate of the circumference of the earth was nearly accurate (it was off by only 200 miles). He proposed that by sailing west from Spain a ship would eventually arrive in India "if there is no large land mass in the way"—this theory was not put to the test until the time of Christopher Columbus!

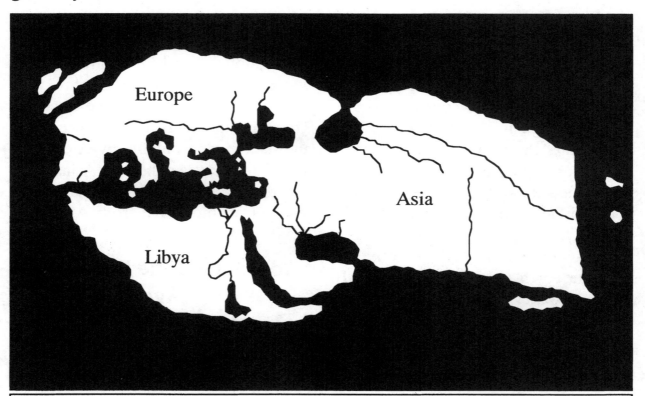

fig. 93 — **The world according to Eratosthenes (c 226 B.C.)**

In the second century B.C. the astronomer Hipparchus of Rhodes (an island off the coast of Ionia) drew a grid of lines on a map of the surface of the earth which were the forerunners of our lines of latitude and longitude. He also charted hundreds of stars.

Ptolemy Sets Back the Clock in Astronomy

Ptolemy (no relation to Alexander's general) studied astronomy in Alexandria in the first century A.D. He wrote a book that described and catalogued the findings of the more important Greek astronomers living from the fifth century B.C. to his own day. Ptolemy refuted the heliocentric theory of Aristarchus and confidently confirmed that the earth was a stationary object encircled by the sun, moon and stars. To his credit, however, is an eight-volume book on geography listing all the known places on the earth and arranging them according to longitude and latitude.

Eureka!

Archimedes is often considered the greatest mathematician of ancient times. He settled in Syracuse (Sicily) after studying in Alexandria. His work in geometry focused primarily on the areas and volumes of curved surfaces. He is well known for his accurate calculation of the ratio of the circumference of a circle to its diameter (called pi). Today middle school students are able to solve their homework problems in geometry because of Archimedes' famous formula.

This imaginative Greek also gained renown for his theory concerning the mass of a body immersed in a liquid. There is a well-known story about how he made his discovery. King Hieron of Syracuse once ordered a crown of gold, but he was worried that not all the gold had been used in the finished product. He therefore asked Archimedes, who had a reputation for being very knowledgeable about scientific matters, to find a means of determining whether he had been cheated by the metalsmith who made the crown. Had the smith melted down a smaller proportion of gold allotted for the crown than he should have, replacing some of the precious metal with silver? Archimedes wondered how he could discover the amount of gold used, but he was baffled.

Later, as he stepped into his bath, the ever-curious mathematician observed the amount of water that spilled over the rim of the tub when he sat down; he estimated that it was equal to the space taken up by his own body in the bath waters. He also noticed that the water overflowed less when he was submerged. On the spot he formulated a rule about water displacement known as Archimedes' Principle: A submerged body displaces an amount of water equal to its volume (density). According to legend, when Archimedes realized he could apply his new-found knowledge to solve the problem of the crown he jumped out of the tub and ran naked through the streets shouting, "Eureka!" (I've found it!).

Soon afterwards he used his principle to determine the amount of gold in the crown. He knew that a certain weight of silver had more volume (was denser) than a similar weight of gold. Therefore, according his principle, the silver should displace more water than a similar weight of gold. When Archimedes submerged the crown in a basin, he noticed that it did indeed displace more water than a golden bar of the same weight. The smith had cheated the king!

Archimedes had a number of practical inventions. One was the water screw, a device used to pump water into irrigation ditches and out of flooded mines. It is still used in developing countries today. He also wrote a detailed explanation of the function of a lever.

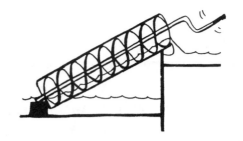

fig. 94 — **Archimedes' water screw**

The Medical Advances of Hippocrates

At first the Greeks believed that disease was caused by the anger of the gods, and the early Greek doctors were the priests of Asclepius, the god of healing. When a person became ill, he went to a temple of Asclepius and made a sacrifice; afterwards the temple priests offered him medicines (few of which worked) and magical charms. In many cases a "patient" was allowed to spend the night at the temple, sleeping on the skins of sacrificed animals. If he was lucky, Asclepius would magically appear in a dream and tell him how he could be cured! Actually, a priest impersonated the god, but the power of suggestion often made the patient believe that he would recover. Many maladies are aggravated by tension and worry, and so by helping the person to relax the priest could relieve any discomfort that was caused by anxiety. People who were seriously ill, of course, would find no cure for their sufferings at the temple.

Hippocrates, who lived in the fourth century B. C., was a scientist who sought to separate the practice of medicine from religious beliefs. He studied the symptoms of his patients and looked for a physical cause for their afflictions. He experimented with various herbal medications, carefully monitoring their effects. He kept a detailed record of his patients' progress and used the data to help other people suffering from similar diseases. He came to the conclusion that a sound diet, proper hygiene and rest were essential for recuperation. They also were the keys to good health.

Hippocrates created a school of medicine on the island of Kos, and he established high ethical standards for his students. He believed that a doctor should be honest with his patient and keep matters pertaining to his case confidential; furthermore, he should do everything possible to protect and preserve human life. These ideals are embodied in the Hippocratic Oath (see Appendix, p. 212), a professional creed that was administered to young doctors until quite recently. Today many medical schools are using alternative oaths, because they consider some of the premises of Hippocrates outdated.

Other Studies of Human Anatomy

In the third century B.C. Greek scientists in Alexandria were fascinated by the discoveries made by Egyptians in the preparation of mummies, and they began to dissect and study the bodies of deceased human beings. Herophilus identified the major organs, and he discovered the difference between veins and arteries. His greatest contribution to medicine was his discovery that the brain is the center of the nervous system (the Egyptians had thought that the center of thought and emotion was the heart!).

Questions:

1. Why did most scientific discoveries take place beyond the mainland of Greece?
2. What was Thales' most important contribution to science?
3. What was Democritus' theory of the composition of matter?
4. What is the Pythagorean Theorem?
5. On what issue did Aristarchus disagree with his mentor, Aristotle?
6. What discovery caused Archimedes to leap from the bathtub in delight?
7. Who was Asclepius?
8. What is the Hippocratic Oath?

Ideas to Think About:

1. Asclepius was the son of Apollo. He was brought up by a centaur (a creature that was half man, half horse) who taught him about medicine. Athena gave the young Asclepius two bottles of magic blood: The blood in one bottle would kill anything, while that in the other could bring the dead back to life. As it turned out, Asclepius frequently used the second bottle and brought so many people back to life that Hades complained to Zeus. Zeus killed Asclepius with a thunderbolt (he was only a demi-god and so he was mortal), but the Olympian later changed his mind and restored Asclepius to life, making him an immortal god.

Asclepius' daughter Hygeia became the goddess of health, and she is the source of our word "hygiene." His other daughter was Panacea (today a panacea is a "cure-all" medicine).

Statues of Asclepius often show him holding a snake (a symbol of regeneration). A snake-entwined staff, called the caduceus, is the symbol of the modern medical profession.

2. Galen was a Greek surgeon living in Rome in the second century A.D. who had studied in Alexandria. He discovered that blood flows through the arteries (earlier scientists had thought that air flowed through them) and his work led to an understanding of how blood circulates throughout the human body.

3. The Greeks had tax-financed medical treatment. This was the world's first medicare!

4. Despite the advances made in medicine, many people continued to rely upon superstition and magic when they were ill or wounded. Common remedies of the Hellenistic Age included the following: for a fever, swallow the blood from the ear of an ass, or else the liver of a cat that was killed when the moon was waning; for a broken bone, apply the ashes of a pig's jaw; for a broken rib, apply the dung of a goat mixed with old wine.

fig. 95 — **A caduceus**

5. Aspirin dates back to the ancient Greeks. Hippocrates noted that a brew of willow leaves, which contain salicin (an ingredient of aspirin), was helpful as a pain-killer in childbirth. (*Salix* is the Latin name for willow.)

Projects:

1. Thales of Miletus was often taunted by his neighbors who thought he was too intellectual. In order to show that he had a practical side, he studied the climate of the island of Lesbor and determined that there would be a bumper crop of olives that season. Then he bought up all the local olive presses! How did this prove that his head was not "in the clouds"? What did he gain from his action?

2. Draw a right triangle of any dimension. Then test the Pythagorian theorem (the square of the longest side of a right triangle equals the squares of the other two sides). Does it work? If not, try again!

3. Ptolemy proposed a geocentric theory of the universe. Using your knowledge of Greek roots and the information you've read about Ptolemy, define the word "geocentric."

4. Life at Pythagoras' school was spartan, to say the least! Find out more about the strict rules regarding food, drink and morals, and write a short report.

5. Read the Hippocratic Oath in the Appendix. Which ideas are still valuable and meaningful in today's world? Which sections of the oath seem outdated?

Chapter XX — THE GREEK LEGACY

The Romans conquered Greece in the second century B.C. and made it a province of their own rapidly expanding empire; over the next hundred years Roman legions gradually subdued the armies of all the nations surrounding the Mediterranean, which they arrogantly referred to as "our sea" (*Mare Nostrum*).

There was a great difference between the highly sophisticated Greeks and their brash, militaristic overlords. Fortunately, the Romans appreciated and valued the rich civilization of the people they had conquered, and they made great efforts to assimilate many aspects of it into their own more primitive culture. In fact, they sent their own children to Athens to receive their formal education. Later, the Roman scholar Horace would write, "Greece the captive enthralled her savage captor!" The Olympian gods were given Roman names and credentials, the life-like Hellenic statues were copied by Italian sculptors, and the theories and principles formulated by Greek scientists were applied to produce great feats of Roman engineering. Greek poets from Homer to Meleager inspired Roman writers, and they in turn would greatly influence later English bards.

In their new role as teachers of the nation that had conquered them, the Greeks were able to perpetuate much of the extraordinary civilization we have been studying. At the same time, their way of life was brought by the Romans to societies in Africa and Europe that had not previously been touched by Alexander.

Our debt to the Greeks is immeasurable. As we conclude our study of their ancient culture, let's take time to consider what made this people unique among the early inhabitants of the Mediterranean world. What special qualities enabled them to achieve such incredible heights in a relatively short period of time? Optimism, of course, and a lively curiosity are characteristics that immediately spring to mind. And the Greeks were certainly resourceful! The early farmers had to work hard to scratch out a living on their rocky peninsula, each man depending upon his various abilities to support himself and his family. From this humble beginning evolved the Greek ideal of competency in many aspects of life, but "nothing in excess."

Pride in their accomplishments led

the Greeks to create a family of gods modeled upon the human race. Their gentle mockery of the human-like weaknesses of the Olympians was, perhaps, their way of laughing at themselves. Such irreverence was not seen in other parts of the ancient world; indeed, the Babylonians lay prostrate upon the ground before statues of their god Marduk, and the Egyptians devoted their lives to serving their god-kings, the pharaohs. The colorful figures of Greek mythology have entertained audiences for over two thousand years, and the lessons that they teach are timeless.

The Greeks knew that a meaningful life began with an understanding of one's self, and generations of poets and philosophers thoroughly explored the complexities of human desires and emotions. A firm belief in the worth of the individual led logically to a love of individual freedom. While other peoples were ruled by absolute monarchs, Athenian citizens considered personal liberty a birthright. Laws had been formulated and written down by earlier societies, but the Greeks were the first to devise a form of government that catered to the needs of the common people. Ironically, the Greek city-states cherished their freedom so much they were never able to be effectively united

as a single nation except in times of war. Nor did ancient Greece ever have a capital city.

While their civilization flourished, the Greeks' celebration of the human potential knew no bounds. They were convinced that man, with his superior intellect, could create order out of the chaos of nature, just as he had established a harmonious society within his own species. "Man is the measure of all things," said the philosopher Protagoras, taking this confidence in human endeavor a step further by implying that the objects of the physical world existed according to how man perceived them!

The Greek spirit is still very much alive today. That ancient standard of self-mastery and quiet courage during difficult times remains the mark of a highly civilized man, a person of "class." And think about those imaginative people of the ancient world the next time you see a graceful pillar, listen to a congressman on television, attend a play, compete in a footrace, recognize the symbol for FTD florists, admire a statue, solve a problem in geometry, or simply marvel at the achievements of mankind. After all these years, Greek aspirations and accomplishments remain a vital part of the modern age.

Projects:

1. Make a collage. Using five or six magazines, look for pictures or words that seem to have something to do with ancient Greece. These can include a picture of a beautiful woman that reminds you of Aphrodite or Helen, an ad for Ajax cleanser (Ajax was one of the Greek kings who went to Troy), a photograph of a house with pillars, a Ford Taurus (remember the Minotaur?), an athlete in action, or a word (such as psychology) that has Greek roots. Be imaginative! Cut out the pictures (and words) you select and glue them on a piece of poster board.

2. Write a newspaper. This is a group project. Select a period or event in Greek history, such as the Persian Wars or the death of Socrates. Then think of the general areas that are covered in daily newspapers: headlines, sports, gossip column, local events, entertainment, books, and don't forget advertising. Political cartoons are always an asset. Decide on a name for your newspaper (the Theban Times, the Athenian Herald, etc.). Assign each member of the group to cover one area. Once the articles and illustrations have been drafted, plan your layout. Cut and paste until you have your page (or pages) arranged to your satisfaction, and then xerox copies of your newspaper of ancient Greece. Hand them out to your classmates and wait for the rave reviews!

3. Make a list of the ways that the civilization of ancient Greece continues to influence the modern world.

Appendix

Excerpts from the Speech of Pericles on the Occasion of the Funeral of Athenian Soldiers Killed during the Peloponnesian War

I will not talk about the battles we have won. I will not talk about how our ancestors became great. Instead, I will talk about our spirit and our way of life. I will talk about those things that have made us great.

Our government does not copy those of our neighbors. Instead, ours is a model for them. Ours is a democracy. The power is in the hands of the people. It is not in the hands of a small group. Everyone is equal before the law. We do not care what class a man belongs to. We care only about his ability. No one is kept from taking part in government because he is poor.

Our political life is free and open. So is our day-to-day life. We do not care if our neighbors enjoy themselves in their own way. We are free and tolerant. But in public affairs we obey the laws. We especially obey the ones that protect the lowly.

Here is another point. When our work is done, we enjoy our free time. There are ceremonies and contests all year. In our homes there is beauty and taste. Our city brings us good things from all over the world.

And our city is open to the whole world. We never keep people out for fear they will spy on us. We have no secrets. We do not rely on trickery. We rely on our own hearts and hands. We are brave in facing danger. Our love of beauty does not lead to weakness. Our love of mind does not make us soft.

Everyone here is interested in the polis.

We do not say those who are not interested in politics are minding their own business. We say they have no business here at all!

Looking at everything, I say Athens is a school for the whole of Greece. Future ages will wonder at us. The present age wonders at us now. Everywhere we have left memorials of our greatness. For this great city of ours, these men fought and died. Each of us who still lives should gladly work for our great city.

I could tell you what we gain by defeating our enemies. Instead, I would rather have you gaze on Athens' greatness every day. Then you would fall in love with our city. You would realize Athens' greatness.

Make up your minds to this. Our happiness depends on our freedom. And our freedom depends on our courage. Because of that, I will not mourn the dead. In their lives, happiness and death went hand in hand.

Abraham Lincoln's Gettysburg Address

Fourscore and seven years ago our fathers brought forth on this continent a new nation, conceived in liberty and dedicated to the proposition that all men are created equal. Now we are engaged in a great civil war, testing whether that nation or any nation so conceived and so dedicated can long endure. We are met on a great battlefield of that war. We have come to dedicate a portion of that field as a final resting-place for those who here gave their lives that that nation might live. It is altogether fitting and proper that we should do this. But in a larger sense, we cannot dedicate, we cannot consecrate, we cannot hallow this ground. The brave men, living and dead, who struggled here have consecrated it far above our poor power to add or detract. The world will little note nor long remember what we say here, but it can never forget what they did here. It is for us, the living, rather to be dedicated here to the unfinished work which they who fought here have thus far so nobly advanced. It is rather for us to be here dedicated to the great task remaining before us—that from these honored dead we take increased devotion to that cause for which they gave the last full measure of devotion—that we here highly resolve that these dead shall not have died in vain, that this nation under God shall have a new birth of freedom, and that government of the people, by the people, and for the people shall not perish from the earth.

The Hippocratic Oath

I swear by Apollo the physician and Aesclepius and health and all-heal and all the gods and goddesses that according to my ability and judgment I will keep this oath and this stipulation: to reckon him who taught me this art equally dear to me as my parents, to share my substance with him and relieve his necessities, if required, to look upon his offspring in the same footing as my own brothers and to teach them his art if they shall wish to learn it without fee or stipulation and that by precept, lecture, and every other mode of instruction I will impart a knowledge of the art to my own sons and those of my teachers and to disciples bound by a stipulation and oath according to the law of medicine, but none to others.

I will follow that system of regimen which, according to my ability and judgment, I consider for the benefit of my patients, and abstain from whatever is deleterious and mischievous. I will give no deadly medicine to any one if asked nor suggest any such counsel, and in like manner I will not give to a woman a pessary to produce abortion. With purity and with holiness I will pass my life and practice my art, I will not cut persons laboring under the stone but will leave this to be done by men who are practitioners of this work. Into whatever houses I enter, I will go into them for the benefit of the sick and will abstain from every voluntary act of mischief and corruption, and further, from the seduction of females or males, of freemen and slaves. Whatever, in connection with my professional practice, or not in connection with it, I see or hear, in the life of men, which ought not to be spoken of abroad, I will not divulge as reckoning that all such should be kept secret.

While I continue to keep this oath unviolated, may it be granted to me to enjoy life and the practice of the art, respected by all men, in all times, but should I trespass and violate this oath, may the reverse be my lot.

Guide to Pronunciation

Achaean — **a-kē´an**
Achilles — **a-kil´ēz**
Acropolis — **a-crŏ´pō-lis**
Aegean — **e-jē´an**
Aeschylus — **es´-kī-lus**
agora — **ăg´o-ra**
Alcibiades — **al-si-bī´i-dēz**
Anatolia — **an-atōl´ia**
Anaxagoras — **an-aks-ag´o-ras**
Anaximander — **a-nak-si-man´der**
Aphrodite — **a-fro-dī´te**
Apollo — **a-pŏl´o**
Archimedes — **ar-ki-mē´dēz**
archon — **ar´kon**
arete — **a-rē´tē**
Aristarchus — **ar-is-tar´kus**
Aristophanes — **ar-is-tof´a-nez**
Aristotle — **ar-is-tŏ´tul**
Boeotia — **bē-ō´sha**
Bucephalus — **bu-sef´a-lus**
Cerberus — **ser´ber-us**
Charon — **kar´on**
chiton — **kī´ton**
Cleisthenes — **klīs´the-nēz**
Cronus — **krō´nus**
Cyrus — **sī´rus**
Darius — **dar-ī´us**
Delphi — **del´fī**
Delos — **dē´lōs**
Draco — **drā´ko**
Ecclesia — **e-klē´si-a**
Eratosthenes — **er-a-tŏs´the-nez**
Euboea — **ū-bē´a**
Euclid — **ū´klid**
Euripides — **u-rĭp´i-dez**
Pheidippides — **fih-dip´i-dez**
Gaea — **jē´a**
Hephaestus — **he-fes´tus**
Herodotus — **her-od´o-tus**
Hippocrates — **hi-pŏk´ra-tez**

Iliad — **il´i-ad**
Ionia — **i-ōn´ia**
Iphegenia — **i-fi-gā´nia**
Issus — **ĭs´us**
Homer — **hō´mer**
Knossos — **nŏs´us**
Leonidas — **le-ōn´i-das**
Lyceum — **li-sē´um**
Lycurgus — **li-ker´gus**
Menelaus — **men-e-lā´us**
Miletus — **mil-ē´tus**
Milo — **mī´lō**
Miltiades — **mil-tē´ah-dez**
Minoan — **mĭ´no-an**
Minos — **mĭ´nos**
Mycenae — **mi-sē´nē**
Mycenaeans — **mi´su-nē´uns**
Odyssey — **ŏd´i-si**
pancratium — **pan-krā´shum**
Pausanias — **po-sā´ni-as**
Peisistratus — **pī-sis´tra-tus**
Peloponnese — **pĕl´o-po-nēs´**
Pericles — **per´i-klez**
Plato — **plā´to**
Pnyx — **niks**
polis — **pō´lis**
Ptolemy — **tŏl´e-mi**
Pythagoras — **pi-thăg´o-ras**
Salamis — **săl´a-mis**
Socrates — **sŏk´ra-tēz**
Solon — **sō´lon**
Sophocles — **sŏf´o-klēz**
Thales — **thā´lez**
Themistocles — **the-mĭs´to-klez**
Thermopylae — **ther-mŏ´pi-lē**
Thucidides — **thu-sĭd´i-dēz**
Xenophon — **zĕn´o-fon**
Xerxes — **zerk´sēz**
Zeus — **zoos**

Suggested Readings

Asimov, Isaac, *The Greeks; A Great Adventure,* Boston: Houghton Mifflin, 1965.

Asimov, Isaac, *Words From The Myths,* Boston: Houghton Mifflin, 1961.

Burrell, Roy, *The Greeks,* New York: Oxford University Press, 1990.

Connolly, Peter, *The Greek Armies,* London: Macdonald Educational, 1977.

Connolly, Peter, *The Greeks,* New York: Oxford University Press, 1990.

Crosher, Judith, *The Greeks,* Morristown, NJ: Silver Burdett, 1985.

D'Aulaire, Ingri and Edgar, *Book of Greek Myths,* New York: Dell, 1992.

Duder, Tessa, *Journey To Olympia,* New York: Scholastic, Inc., 1992.

Etienne, Roland and Francoise, *The Search for Ancient Greece,* New York: Harry N. Abrams, Inc. (Discoveries), 1992.

Evans, Cheryl and Anne Millard, *Greek Myths and Legends,* London: Usborne, 1985.

Gay, Kathlyn, *Science in Ancient Greece,* New York: Franklin Watts, 1988.

Glubok, Shirley and Alfred Tamarin, *Olympic Games in Ancient Greece,* New York: Harper and Row, 1976.

Hamilton, Edith, *The Greek Way,* New York: Time, Inc., 1963.

Hamilton, Edith, *Mythology,* New York: Penguin Books, 1989.

Jones, John Ellis, *History as Evidence; Ancient Greece,* New York: Warwick Press, 1983.

Macrone, Michael, *It's Greek to Me!,* New York: Harper Collins, 1991.

Miquel, Pierre, *Life in Ancient Greece,* Morristown, NJ: Silver Burdett, 1985.

Picard, Barbara, *The Odyssey of Homer,* New York: Oxford University Press, 1991.

Peach, Susan and Anne Millard, *The Greeks,* London: Usborne Publishing Ltd., 1990.

Powell, Anton, *Cultural Atlas for Young People: Ancient Greece,* New York: Facts on File, 1989.

Wepman, Dennis, *Alexander the Great,* New York: Chelsea House, 1986.

Recommended Videos: *Alexander the Great: Clash of the Titans; In Search of Troy*

Index